Malla Moe
and
Her Gospel Wagon

MALLA MOE
AND HER
GOSPEL WAGON

DOROTHY MARTIN

MOODY PRESS

CHICAGO

Copyright © 1985 by
The Moody Bible Institute
of Chicago

Library of Congress Cataloging in Publication Data

Martin, Dorothy.
   Malla Moe and her gospel wagon.

   1. Moe, Malla.   2. Missionaries--South Africa--
Biography.   3. Missionaries--United States--Biography.
I. Title.
BV3625.S672M645 1985   266'.0092'4 [B]   85-5007
ISBN 0-8024-5166-7 (pbk.)

1 2 3 4 5 6 7 Printing/PC/Year 90 89 88 87 86 85

1

"Hey! Come back, you dumb sheep."

Malla dashed for the lamb teetering on the edge of the sharp drop of the hill. "Silly thing," she scolded lovingly. "Don't you know you'll kill yourself?"

Malla stretched out on the grass again, her arms under her head. The summer sun was warm on her face as she stared up at the soft clouds, white against the blue sky. They looked as fluffy as the sheep grazing over the hillside. No country could possibly be more beautiful than Norway.

"This is the best time of the whole year—when I don't have to struggle with school," she explained to the big ram, who ignored her as he chewed grass.

Even the two days a week that school met were too much for Malla when there was so much to see and do out of doors, summer and winter. No book could tell her where to find the nests the rabbits hid or tell her which bird was trilling its song over her head. She hated to waste time indoors when she could be riding bareback across the fields, splashing across rivers, or climbing to the top of a tree to see how far the world reached.

Malla stretched. Two more years and she would be fifteen and through with school forever. Why did she need more education than that? Where would she ever go that would require more education? "I love it right here, even if our town is small. I don't ever want to leave it."

Malla sat up then and put her arms around her knees, her forehead creasing in a frown. Turning fifteen meant that she would have to join the church. She would have to face the hard questions that had been churning in her mind ever since she could remember—or at least since she had been eight years old. She thought about the day her mother had said, "Malla, do you know that you have a baby brother and two baby sisters in heaven?"

Her questions had tumbled out. "Why? Did they want to go? How did they get there? What do they do, Mother? Will—will I have to go to heaven, too?"

Her mother hadn't really answered the questions. She had only said, "You must pray to Jesus to take you there." But that hadn't helped at all. And the stories her mother had told her about how Jesus had suffered and died for her had not helped either.

As she stared out across the meadow, Malla remembered those evangelistic meetings she had gone to. The minister had preached in such a different way from the ministers in the State church. One of her friends had mocked the people who attended the meetings. "Look how plain they dress. The women look so drab. They don't wear any ribbons or lace. And they don't ever laugh."

The people did laugh, but Malla could tell it was not in the sneering, mocking way of her neighbors. These people never laughed at others or put them down. And they talked very seriously about the Lord Jesus. They talked about God as though He was a friend.

"Even Papa doesn't talk about God and heaven except on Sunday when he's in church," she said to the little lamb who was rubbing against her.

Malla pulled a piece of grass to chew on as she frowned over the questions she knew the minister would ask when she went forward to join the church. His voice would be loud and stern, and his forehead would have a deep frown line as he asked, "Will you give your heart to God? Will you love and serve God instead of the devil?"

"Yes," she said out loud to the silent grass and listening trees. "I want to love God. I want to serve Him. But I don't know how."

The question bothered her the rest of the afternoon, as she ran after the sheep and goats. How could she find out how to serve God? On the way home she decided, "I'll visit Auntie tomorrow, if she's not too sick to talk to me. She is so close to heaven, maybe she can help me."

Doubt gnawed at her as she stood outside her aunt's house the next day. Mother would be cross if Auntie were upset in any way. Then, before she could change her mind, she pushed open the door and called, "Auntie! I've brought you some of Mama's good soup."

Her aunt sipped some of the fragrant broth and then lay back against her pillow. "Dear Malla," she whispered. "I have been thinking so much about you. You know how sick I have been. And now I am going to heaven. Will you go with me?"

"But—I don't want to die yet." Sudden fear swept her at the thought.

She felt her aunt's thin fingers tighten on hers as she whispered, "Dear Malla. Please promise to meet me in heaven."

Malla struggled for words, wanting to please her aunt and yet afraid to say yes to something she was so uncertain about. Then, as she looked at her aunt's thin face and pleading eyes, she understood. Auntie wasn't talking about going to heaven right now but about surrendering completely to God. Malla knew she wasn't ready to do that, but she had to say something to make her aunt happy.

"Yes, Auntie," she whispered, squeezing her aunt's hand. "I will meet you in heaven." To herself she added, *Somehow I'll find out how to get there.*

But as the months went by she forgot her promise. She found it hard to think about God. Most of her friends were more interested in going to parties than in going to church. "How come you always want to talk about God?" they demanded. "There's time enough for that when you get old. Now is the time to have fun."

So, when she was seventeen, Malla decided she was not going to be the only one who was left out of all the fun. The glimmer she had had of living a different kind of life slipped away as she went partying with her friends. She came home late one evening, hoping to slip in quietly without her mother's hearing and scolding. But a light in the kitchen made her peek into the room. She saw her mother sitting at the table, her face streaked with tears, her hands twisting her apron.

"Malla—your father—he's so sick. I'm afraid he's going to—" She burst into tears and flung her apron over her head.

"I knew he didn't feel well, but—oh, Mama, is he going to die?"

Her mother only sobbed louder, nodding her head without answering. Malla ran to the bedroom and found her father tossing restlessly. His voice was thin and whispery as he said, "Malla, call everyone. I must—talk."

"Wait until morning, Papa."

"No. May be—too late. I am—already—late."

With his six children kneeling around the bed and his voice fading with weakness, he said, "Children, give your hearts to God. I—beg you. My example—not good. I was—afraid. Everyone looked up to me. I could not—humble myself—say I needed to know God—better. Dear children—you can. You still have time. Believe in Jesus."

His words were a blow to Malla as she thought of the way she was living. She rushed from the room, stumbling across the kitchen and out into the night. She slipped into the barn and cried, "God—please forgive me, and give me just a little bit of your salvation and your joy."

Almost before her rush of words stopped, she knew her prayer was heard. "I'll never turn my back on You again, God. Not for anything or anyone."

Soon after her father's death a minister came to town to hold revival meetings. Going to the meeting and hearing the singing and preaching helped Malla keep her resolve. She went knocking on doors to invite people to the meetings and found herself happier than she had ever been.

Then suddenly her mother became ill. Knowing how sick she was, she begged Malla, "Please take care of Dorothea. She is only twelve, not able to care for herself the way you can at nineteen. Promise me you will look after her until she is grown."

Malla promised, not knowing how she could carry out the promise. What kind of job could she get? She had no education to be a teacher. Not only had her school training been inferior, but she had wasted the years she had been there.

"I still want to serve you in some way, God," she prayed. "I want to do something for you. But how can I? I'm not smart enough to be a teacher or a missionary. And I'm too old now to go back to

9

school. The church will never send out an untrained person, especially a woman. And now I have Dorothea to take care of."

The days that followed were a jumble of restlessness, as her prayers seemed to go unanswered.

Then a letter came from a married sister in America. "Come to America," Karin wrote. "You and Dorothea can stay with us, and we can find you a job doing housework. You need not feel ashamed to do housework. Americans like to hire girls from our country, because they know we clean and cook good. You can learn English and earn money besides. We can get Dorothea into a school here and let her train for a good job. Do come, Malla."

Malla jumped at the chance, and she and Dorothea sailed for America. The size and noise and rush of Chicago overwhelmed them—especially Dorothea, who clung to Karin for safety. "You'll get used to so many people," Karin promised.

It was crowded in Karin's house, but Dorothea went to school, and Malla found a job right away doing housework. She listened carefully to the people in the family as they talked, and she tried to twist her tongue to make the unaccustomed, strange-sounding words. The noise and rush and dirt of Chicago bothered her. Worst of all no one, including Karin and her husband, seemed to have time for God. And they were impatient at her longing for Christian friends.

Finally, on her own, she decided to find a church where she could feel at home. Her job as a housemaid meant evening work, which kept her from going to some meetings she saw advertised. She impulsively quit her job and got another one in a laundry on the North Side of Chicago, near a church. She went to the service on Sunday and slipped shyly into a seat at the back of the auditorium. As she looked timidly around, she heard a man's voice exclaim, "Malla Moe! Is that you?"

She looked up at the beaming face of the man standing before her with outstretched hands. "You are here in America, Malla? What a surprise!"

She stared back at him, her face blank. Then recognition came, and she jumped up. "You held meetings in our home. Papa invited you, and we sat all of us around. You preached to us on God's love. Oh, I never forgot what you said. How much it meant to me! But—how do you remember me?"

He took her hands in his and said simply, "I remember how hungry you looked and how unhappy, as though you were searching, searching. You have found God and His love?"

"Oh, yes! And I want to serve Him now. Is there something I can do for Him here in Chicago? I know so little English to speak."

"We have a Sunday school class of girls who need a teacher. They have come from the old country as you have. They will be able to understand you. You need only to tell them of Jesus. I am sure you will find words for that."

Malla not only taught the girls each Sunday but visited each one in her home and talked to the parents about Jesus.

She also went often to the services at Moody Church on Chicago Avenue. She liked the variety of speakers and especially enjoyed listening to Dwight L. Moody. At the close of one meeting she felt his hand on her shoulder. In his usual abrupt manner he asked, "Are you saved?"

"Yes." Her answer was quick and positive.

"Then why don't you go to work?" His question was accompanied by a quick impatient shove. "God

11

has urgent work waiting. Get busy on God's business."

The command intensified her desire to serve God. She tried to follow Moody's example and speak to at least one person a day about Christ. But a thought nagged at her constantly. "I can never really serve God. I am so uneducated. I know nothing."

As soon as she finished each long day at the laundry, she ate a quick supper and hurried to church. One day she went to a meeting conducted by Fredrick Franson. He talked about the desperate need of people in other countries to know Christ and told of their hopelessness and despair. Tears filled her eyes and ran down her cheeks. *I was like that,* she thought. *Lost—afraid—lonely—thirsting for God. If only those poor people could know there is rest in the Lord Jesus.*

As she listened to Mr. Franson's appeal for missionaries, she kept up a running conversation with herself. *I don't like the Chinese. I could never go to China. But Africa—that would not be too bad.*

But she knew such thoughts were useless. What mission board would accept her when she had no education? Then there was the promise she had made to her dying mother to look after Dorothea. She could not shove that responsibility onto Karin.

With every excuse she gave, she argued in her own mind, *What if God wants me to go?* Finally, in desperation, she wrote all her questions and longing in a letter and mailed it to Mr. Franson, asking his advice. Every day for weeks she hurried home from work, expecting an answer. When the weeks lengthened into months and no answer came, she felt relief sweep over her. God didn't want her as a missionary after all.

A year later, Malla heard that Mr. Franson was in

Chicago again, looking for volunteers for his new mission society, the Scandinavian Alliance Mission. Malla couldn't stay away from the meetings. She knew the missionary question for her had been settled, so she went just to enjoy the service. At the close, Mr. Franson strode over to her. "God wants you to be a missionary in Africa."

"No! No, I could never go."

"Aren't you the young lady who wrote to me?"

"Yes, but you didn't answer. So I was sure God did not want me."

He shook his head ruefully. "Forgive me for not answering. I was busy. But you can still go."

Malla stumbled out her excuses and hurried from the church. The next evening, Mr. Franson urged her again. "I have heard of your zeal to witness here in Chicago, but Africa needs you much more."

"I have no training. I would have to go to Moody Bible Institute first. And I am too old. I am already twenty-nine. I promised my mother I would take care of my younger sister."

Mr. Franson's voice was warm, but stern, as he said, "God says, 'Go,' and the heathen say, 'Come.' You must go without delay." Then he looked down into her pleading eyes and said gently, "I will pray for you."

That troubled Malla more than ever, knowing his reputation in prayer. He meant he would bring her before God for an answer. The next evening she went to visit a friend. Standing in the hall, she felt as though God's hand were on her shoulder, pushing her out to a place beyond her human ability—a place where she must trust God alone for everything.

She couldn't keep back the words that filled her mind. *What can I say to you, God? I have given myself to you already. If you want me in Africa, I say yes.*

Her family and friends were aghast at the decision. "Malla, you can't do this," Karin protested. "You promised to care for Dorothea, and now you are leaving me with the responsibility. I am working. I can't give her the time she needs."

And Dorothea was bitter, accusing Malla of deserting her. "You promised you would never leave me."

Malla was torn between her commitment to Dorothea and her promise to obey God. "You will have to make them willing to let me go," she told God, almost despairing that He could or would. But almost overnight Karin's attitude changed, and even Dorothea seemed to accept the situation.

Malla had very little time in which to get ready. Mr. Franson gave the candidates a two-week training session filled with Bible study and practical suggestions. He never asked his missionaries how much education they had. He only wanted them to be "filled with the Spirit" and "know how to trust God." He wanted them to have faith in a God who was able to do the impossible.

On April 1, 1892, one week after the training session, the group of three men and five women gathered in New York for their "commissioning." Each of the candidates was asked to share in the service. Malla stood when it was her turn and said in her far from perfect English, "Not easy to talk to so many people. On street I said to God, 'God, give me something to say. You know I know nothing!' He gave me, 'The Lord is my shepherd; I shall not want! That's all. Amen."

When she sat down she saw some people shaking their heads. She was sure they were thinking the same thing she was. How could someone so uneducated, so inarticulate, be a successful missionary?

14

The men in the group all had theological training. One of the women was a nurse; all the others had education and experience working in churches. She had none of those things.

But Mr. Franson nodded with satisfaction as he looked at her. He knew she loved God and wanted to win others to the Lord Jesus. He was satisfied that he had chosen wisely.

As the shoreline of America faded from view, Malla stood with the others at the ship's rail. Mr. Franson's parting words rang in her ears. "Fast and pray. If you are sick, fast and pray; if the language is hard to learn, fast and pray. If the people will not listen to you, fast and pray. If you have nothing to eat, then fast—and pray."

"I will remember," she vowed, as the salt breeze cooled her flushed face and God's peace calmed her beating heart.

2

Malla stood at the ship's railing, the wind whipping her hair and clothes. She preferred the bite of the open air to the stuffy cabin, where the constant motion of the ship was more noticeable and made her stomach lurch. She stared out across the water, her eyes narrowed against the sun and wind, enjoying the colors that shifted from deep blue to stormy gray. She was glad for the six-week-long journey. It was giving her time to think back over the decision she had made so quickly. She wondered if the other members of the small missionary group felt as breathless as she did. Their names slipped through her mind—Emma Homme, Augusta Hultberg, Emelia Forbord, Lizzie Jorgensen, Carl Paulson, Paul Gullander, and Andrew Haugerud. Mr. Franson had appointed Andrew to be the leader of the group.

Malla thought about each of them as she paced the deck. She knew the women, especially, were one in their desire to take the gospel to those in Africa who needed to hear. But they were all so different in their experience and background. Malla frowned, thinking of the sharp retort Emma had made to her suggestion that they spend several hours a day in prayer.

"It is my poor English," Malla said aloud to the waves. "She thought I meant she not pray enough. I must not speak so quick." She nodded her head in agreement when Andrew said, "We must be understanding of our differences, since we will be working so closely together."

They were all glad when the ship finally docked at Durban, South Africa. They had only a brief stop before going to a station of the East Africa Free Mission for language study. They arrived there June 9, 1892, after many miles of inland travel. Even that was not the end, for their ultimate destination was Mashonaland, a thousand miles to the north. Andrew called the group together to discuss plans.

"Mr. Nielsen, of the station here, thinks it best for me to go ahead to Mashonaland and get a station set up before the rest of you come. He has agreed to go with me, which will be a great help. I understand the Mashona don't have a very good reputation for welcoming strangers. And they are looked down on by other tribes."

"Why?" Malla asked.

"They're called 'eaters of dirt,' which I suppose says something about their sanitation habits."

"How long, then, before we come?" Malla burst out, conscious of the disapproval of the other women at her pushing forward. But she didn't care. She hadn't come all this distance so late in life just to sit on the fringe of opportunity.

Andrew shook his head. "I don't know. Months perhaps. We'll have to slog the miles on foot and then wait for permission from the chief to establish a station. Mr. Nielsen says the chiefs are pretty independent, and we might have trouble getting permission."

"We can use the time here," Malla said loudly. "We have much to learn about the language and people." Her words sounded bold, but inside she quaked at the thought of closer contact with the Africans. "God, you teach me to love them," she whispered over and over again. "They smell so bad."

In the midst of getting ready for the survey trip, Andrew asked Malla to marry him when he returned. Malla faced him, struggling with a conflict of emotions, not knowing what to say. Finally she burst out, "I not come all the way to Africa to get married! I come to serve God."

He took her hand, asking gently, "Don't you think you can do both?"

Her usual blunt, direct way of meeting problems deserted her, and she dared not let him see the conflicting emotions that battled inside. She wanted love and marriage, yes, but she had to be sure God wanted that for her.

"Will you think about it while I am gone?" he probed.

"Yah, but I cannot promise I will change." Then she said miserably, "I do not know how God can use me here. These people—so dirty, their way of living— it is disgusting. It is terrible the way the women must work so hard. And so superstitutious they are."

"Isn't that why we came?" Andrew asked. "To change them? I remember reading the biography of Robert Moffat, who worked not far from here. One day one of the men said to him, 'You found us beasts and made us men.' Of course it was God who did it there, and He can do it here as well."

Malla nodded. "I remember Mr. Franson saying good things about Mr. Moffat. I copy down what he say. He tell of 'the smoke of a thousand villages— villages whose people are without Christ, without God, and without hope in the world.' When I hear, my heart hurts. But—"

"Yes?" Andrew prodded when she stopped.

"But I do not expect such dirt—such superstition."

Andrew smiled at her. "Perhaps it will be easier if we share it. I will be gone for months, but when I return, will you have an answer for me?"

Malla nodded, not trusting her voice to speak.

Malla was determined to overcome her dislike of the people and their customs. *When I know them I will like them,* she told herself, hoping that would be true. She decided the best way to know them was to live among them, so one day she and Emma went to live in a kraal—a village within walking distance of the mission station. They set out, carrying a few changes of clothing and their Bibles. Coming to the outskirts, they stopped to look at the circle of huts.

"It looks like an enormous patch of mushrooms!" Emma exclaimed, laughing. In the center of the circle were the cattle and food storage huts. The sleeping huts were built on the outer rim. A series of stakes driven into the ground gave a circle of protection around the grass huts.

"Look at that," Emma said, shaking her head. "The cattle are in the center for the most protection. Apparently Zulu men consider them more valuable than their wives or children."

"What you think the huts like inside?" Malla asked nervously. Then her characteristic boldness came back, and she said, "We go find out."

They walked slowly toward the buildings. Malla glanced at Emma, wondering if she were more nervous than she appeared to be. She watched Emma speak to the chief by using hand signs and stammering out the few words of greeting that Mr. Nielsen had taught them. The chief pointed out the hut where his wives lived, motioning them to go in. They stooped to enter and immediately choked and coughed from the smoke of the wood fire that smoldered in a hollow place scooped out in the middle of the dirt floor. A great iron pot filled with some smelly mess simmered over it.

Malla ducked as her head brushed against objects hanging from the grass roof. She felt her stomach turn over at the chickens pecking noisily around the unwashed cooking pots on the floor and the grunting pig thrusting its snout into the pots. She was used to taking care of animals as a girl, but that had been years ago, and they had not been allowed in the kitchen.

"Ouch!" Malla couldn't stop the exclamation as she felt someone yank her hair, jerking her head back. She whirled to face the young boy standing behind her, a wide grin showing his white teeth. Her frown melted as she understood from his motions that he was curious to know if her long hair was fastened to her head the same way his cropped hair was.

Emma nudged Malla, nodding at the man beckoning to them. "I think he wants us to follow him."

They ducked again to go through the low doorway, little children darting around them, and followed the man to a low hut.

"This must be the one we are to stay in." Emma's voice trembled slightly, and Malla nodded, licking her dry lips. They went in and found it full of young girls, who pointed shyly to the mat in the corner where Malla and Emma were to sleep.

They shook their heads at the food offered them from the cooking pot, and Malla was sure she would throw up any minute. She managed to get down a little of the food she and Emma had brought with them. She listened to the chattering crowd that had pushed into the hut and turned questioningly to their guide. Pointing to their mouths and then to her ears, she asked, "What they say?"

With many gestures and a few words of English, he answered, "They wonder why you come. Why you wander alone with no man to care for you. It not done that way here."

"We come to tell about Jesus. Tell you He loves you." It took so long to make her answer clear that Malla was afraid she had not been understood. Then she saw the scowl that darkened the man's face.

"We have gods!"

"But do they love you?"

"We fear them. Not good to love gods. God must be feared, or he not be powerful."

As they talked, the sun was setting behind the blue and purple haze of the mountains, and suddenly it was completely dark. Malla and Emma fumbled their way to their mat and lay down. There was no light to lift the blanket of darkness. The incessant chirping of crickets and the croaking of frogs sounded loud in the stillness of the African night. *Will I ever get used to this country and these people?* Malla wondered.

She asked herself that question over and over in the next few days. She saw the women burdened with the care of the children, yet filing out every morning to the fields, their bodies bent under the babies' weight. They worked in the fields all day and then came home to cook the evening meal. Most of the time the men sat around the big clay pots drinking beer and taking pinches of snuff.

One day a sudden scream from one of the huts made Malla and Emma look at one another in fear. "What is it?" Emma asked a man passing their hut.

He shrugged. "It is nothing. It is a woman who is to give birth, but the baby will not come. The evil spirit does not want the baby to be born."

Malla ran to the hut and pushed through the watching crowd. The woman's screams made her realize how helpless, how useless, she was. "I not a nurse. I can do nothing to help."

She ran from the hut, the screams following her, and burst into the hut where she and Emma slept. "You were wrong!" she cried out to God. "Why I let You push me to mission field? I know nothing. How can I help these people? I no help when they sick. I not able to talk to them. I too stupid to learn different language."

Emma tried to comfort her, but she turned away. "I pray. I not know how to deliver a child, but I know how to pray."

She fell on her knees in one corner of the hut, burying her face against her arms. She stayed that way, motionless, not aware of the time. Suddenly she felt her heavy burden lift, and she stood up. "Now I eat, Emma. God answers." She turned for some food and heard someone outside the hut call, "The baby is come. The mother is well."

She and Emma went to see the baby and watched intently the unusual customs. The father was not allowed to enter the hut with the baby newly born. But the witch doctor was busy working his magic protections against sickness. Medicine was put into a piece of old rag that was twisted into a tight knot and tied around the baby's neck as a sure charm against the ever watchful evil spirits. Then the lobes of the baby's ears were pierced, and a small stick was pushed through the holes.

"Why you do that?" Malla asked.

"So she will hear well."

Malla and Emma walked slowly back to their hut. "If only we could help them see how useless all that is. But when we don't know the language—" Emma

23

threw out her hands in a hopeless gesture.

Malla burst out, "If it were just to learn and to remember words, I could do that. But the clicking sounds, those I cannot make. Each sound has sounds. Each click—it must turn up, or it must turn down. It must be just so."

"And each one of the sixty-three different sounds has its own separate meaning." Emma's discouragement was clear on her face.

"I get up early every morning at four o'clock. I must have time to study. But it do no good. How can they know of God if we have no words?" The cry in Malla's voice came from her heart. The reason she had come to Africa was to bring people to God. Five months had passed already, and she saw no result.

During Christmas week she went alone to a service at another mission station some distance away. She was so blessed by the reminder of God's love in sending His Son that she couldn't keep from running home. Suddenly she tripped over a branch and fell, and an excruciating pain tore at her. Because she was so seldom sick, she panicked at the thought of lying out in the open by herself with night coming on. She could imagine animals prowling in the bushes and insects feeding on her.

"God—please! Do not let me die out here."

Finally, by crawling part of the way and using a broken stick as a crutch, she managed to reach the kraal where she was staying. The throbbing pain had lessened by morning, but the memory of it stayed with her. She thought of the woman whose childbirth had been so painful and whom she had avoided. Impulsively Malla went to her and by signs and a few words managed to say, "I cry for you. I ask God to bring your baby safe."

She didn't know if the woman understood her

meaning, and she watched her face anxiously. The woman did understand the sympathy in Malla's voice, and tears rolled down her cheeks.

"Why, she cry just like I do." Malla said the words out loud, and they broke the shell Malla had built around herself since coming to Africa. She realized that she had thought of herself as a helper of people less human than herself. She had seen only the difference between them—the dirt and ignorance and superstition. Now she felt a stirring of kinship as she began to understand the suffering in their lives. The women, especially, needed the love and hope that she could show them in Christ.

Her thoughts flew to Andrew. When he came back, if he asked her again to marry him—perhaps—perhaps she would say yes. She had not understood the loneliness of missionary life. It would be good to have someone with whom to share sorrows and joys and to give and receive encouragement.

The thought was a comfort as she went by herself to visit a new kraal during Christmas week and stayed alone in a hut. Doubt came again to make her wonder if the decision to marry Andrew was the one God wanted her to make. Was it right for Andrew as well as for herself? She tossed on her narrow cot, feeling the unease and uncertainty that she always seemed to go through when making decisions.

Then a commotion outside the hut brought her fully awake, and she got up to peer out the low entrance. The full moon lighted the dirt clearing in front of the hut, and she saw a mother hen clucking and flapping her wings as she scurried to gather her chicks in a huddle close to her. Something had apparently disturbed her, and she was concerned for the safety of her little brood. The little chicks' chirping and peeping gradually quieted as they felt their mother's warmth and beating heart.

Malla settled back, the turmoil in her heart quieting. Long ago a preacher in Norway had talked of God's promises being like a mother hen's feathers, providing security and peace.

"Thank You, God," she whispered. "Thank You for showing that You are with me. I trust You always."

3

Even though the little group of missionaries faced the new year of 1893 with uncertainty about their place of service, Malla was sure God would open doors for them. If He did not want them in Mashonaland, then He would open another place. She had not told anyone of Andrew's proposal, keeping it as a loving shroud around her. A letter came from him the first of February.

"Good news!" he wrote. "God has opened a door in Swaziland where very little Christian work is being done. I am sure we will all feel at rest here, as there are many people who do not know the Savior. It is a beautiful spot with plenty of food and water. I believe God has at last brought us to the place where He wants us to work. From where I stand right now on the top of a hill, I can see fourteen kraals hidden away in the hills where there is no gospel witness."

Malla took the letter to read again in private, even though it had nothing personal for her in it. Once again she felt her mind tumbling with questions, and her heart filled with doubts about the answer she must give Andrew when he returned.

A month later a letter came from Mr. Nielsen which bluntly settled those doubts. Andrew, burning with fever when he had written his letter, had died. He was buried there in Swaziland just six months

27

after his arrival in Africa.

Malla stumbled away to be by herself. Since none of the others knew of Andrew's proposal, she did not want them questioning the intensity of her grief.

"God, why you do this?" she pleaded. "The future looks so black. Of the three men who came out, you know Carl Paulson remains in Durban. Paul Gullander not want to be leader. Now you take Andrew. What we do now? You have bring us so far for nothing?"

After consultation and prayer, the group made plans to move to Swaziland. They hired a Norwegian transport rider to travel with them and followed his advice to wait until June, a winter month, to avoid contracting fever on the way. Then, at the end of May, Mrs. Gullander gave birth to twins, and her husband decided they should wait until she was well enough to travel.

Malla, Lizzie, and Emma looked at one another in dismay. That left the women with no man to give direction to the work and make contact with the chiefs of the kraals, who might not want to deal with women.

"We should ask that young Englishman we meet in Durban. That nice Mr. Dawson," Malla suggested.

Emma frowned. "Well—of course, he isn't a missionary."

But Mr. Nielsen nodded his head approvingly. "He does work for the East Africa Mission in his spare time. And he is feeling lonely since his wife died recently. He might be willing to help out temporarily."

Mr. Dawson did agree to travel with the women. "I'll stay long enough to help you build the house you need. After all, that is my trade. And I'll see that you get a crop in before I leave."

Malla felt her heart beating with excitement on May 31, 1893, as the tiny procession of wagons pulled out and headed for Swaziland, far to the north. She had to control her desire to shout, telling herself sternly, *At thirty, you must be quiet.*

But her sense of high adventure made even the dangerous matter of fording swollen rivers, with the water lapping at the wagon bottoms and now and then sloshing inside, something to enjoy rather than fear. Each day brought a new experience.

As they stopped on the fifth night to unhitch the oxen and circle the wagons for safety, a shout came from one of the African helpers.

"Someone comes from behind. A white man."

They rushed to meet the man, who spurred his horse toward the wagons. It was Paul Gullander, his eyes red-rimmed from anguish and sleeplessness. His face crumpled with emotion as he blurted, "Augusta— the doctors couldn't save her. I came to tell you. I will go to Swaziland with you to see you safely settled. Then I must go back and take my babies home to Sweden."

Malla listened with the others, tears of sorrow streaming down her cheeks. They were all stunned at another seeming victory for Satan. Four of the eight who had come in answer to God's call were gone before they had been in the country a year. If God had really called them, wouldn't He have taken care of them? It must be they were mistaken. It must be as she had thought before—Mr. Franson had sent them out, not God.

Go back, came an insistent whisper. *Go back before you die too.*

She turned away from the others, walking restlessly back and forth. She reached automatically for her Bible. As she did, she remembered the chapter in

29

Jonah that she had read that morning for her devotions. A faint smile quirked her lips, as a stray thought came. *If I run away, will God have a big fish ready to swallow me?*

The thought brought release from the net of discouragement. God had answered her prayers through those long years of searching for Him. He had sent her here. She would trust Him.

This victory and the expectancy of what God would do carried her through the remaining five weeks of travel. The small group set up camp for the last time on July 6, knowing that in a few days they must say good-bye to Paul, with whom they had shared so many experiences in that brief year. But the sadness of the good-bye was swallowed up in the rush to construct the buildings and get settled. Under Mr. Dawson's directions, the women became as skilled as the men in mixing the mud for the buildings.

"We do as good as the Africans," Malla said, oozing her hands through the mud and plastering it on the simple frame Mr. Dawson had made.

But Malla was restless and eager to contact people. "I go to a kraal this afternoon, Emma. You come too?"

"No." Emma looked at her and then quickly away. "I, uh—I think I'll stay here. I want to study the language."

"Is better to study by practicing on people. When I read from Zulu Bible, Swazi people understand. Come with me," Malla urged.

When Emma shook her head, Malla went alone, wondering why Emma didn't seem interested in going to the kraals since they had moved to Swaziland. As she walked along the narrow, uneven trail, she practiced reading aloud from the Bible. Her regret at being uneducated made her determined to study hard. She had to overcome her fear of the people, especially the men, as they stood scowling at her, holding their spears and shields. The only way to overcome that fear was to get to know them. And the only way to do that was to be with them in their kraals.

Another anxiety grew as the buildings were finished and the day approached when Mr. Dawson would leave them. What would she and Emma and Emelia and Lizzie do when they were left alone?

The answer didn't seem like an answer when it came. Mr. Dawson announced that he and Emma were engaged. Malla looked at Emma's blushing face, realizing now why Emma had stayed at the station so often instead of going to visit the kraals. Remembering her feelings about Andrew, she understood.

"We are going back to Durban to be married and wait for God's direction as to what He wants us to do," Mr. Dawson finished.

The three remaining members of the original eight Scandinavian Alliance missionaries to Africa looked at one another in silence. Then Malla said, at first slowly and then with a rush of confidence, "We just three, but God is with us. He once tell prophet Elisha that he not alone. More were with him than with enemy. Then He let Elisha see whole army of angels around him. We have army of protection too. It is God."

Malla meant the words she said so bravely, but it still was hard to say good-bye to Emma and Mr. Dawson as they climbed into the wagon for the return trip to Durban. They would miss Mr. Dawson's skill in building and his knowledge of the language. More than once he had kept them from bringing down a chief's wrath on them by supplying the right word.

"Yah, and the way he sings. So beautiful," Malla said. She knew she would miss Emma's good sense and skills, even though they so often disagreed on the way to do things.

Malla was overwhelmed by loneliness as she watched the wagon creak along the narrow path, and she waved until it was lost to sight. God had called her to be a missionary; she was sure of that. And she was committed to staying as a single missionary. But the commitment didn't keep away the helpless feelings that gripped her. Nothing she did brought happiness. She didn't see any results to her stammering efforts to talk to the people about God. Her language was so limited. The people were polite and responsive to the simple things she did to help them physically. Her nursing skills were skimpy but sufficient to bandage cuts and treat sores. But when she tried to talk to them about their customs, they twisted everything she said.

When she asked, "Why you throw dust in the air?" they shrugged and replied, "It is the custom."

"Why your women do all the work?" The inevitable shrug and reply — "It is the custom."

"You teach children politeness," she said one day to the headman of a kraal. "But you not teach not to lie. Why?"

He stared back at her, his face creased by a puzzled frown. "A lie is not a lie unless it is discovered," he answered.

Malla shook her head in despair when talking to Lizzie one day. "Whoever say Africans stupid never live with them. Never talk with them. They very clever at twisting words when I talk about things. Especially when I talk about God. I so wish I had more education."

"Malla, you are always saying that," Lizzie replied impatiently. "But you know God's Word. That's what they need."

"I know. So—I have decided. I not just visit kraal one day or two or one week. I go live there."

"Malla! Don't be foolish. You can't go and live in a kraal by yourself."

"I can. I have talked to Mahahane—you remember him, Lizzie? We talked one day in that kraal over beyond trees. I ask could I have hut to sleep in for one month. He say yes, if I bring own food and cooking pot. The kraal is not so far away. I come back if I have to."

Malla knew that Lizzie and Emelia objected because they were worried about her safety. "God gave idea; God go with me," she insisted. So she began to make plans for the walk to the kraal. She hired two young African boys she thought she could trust to carry her cooking pot, food, and folding cot. She decided to take gifts for the headman and his wives and asked Lizzie's and Emelia's advice. They helped her put together a supply of sugar, matches, salt, and bits of colored cloth, all the while trying to persuade her to change her mind.

"This just experiment," she insisted. "If it not work, I not do it again."

She was nervous when she set out on the walk to the kraal late one afternoon. But as she went along the narrow path, she felt her spirits lift. Even when night fell suddenly, the darkness was lighted by a beautiful full moon. She knew it was the same beautiful moon that had shone down on her so often when she was a young girl in Norway. She wasn't alone. God was with her.

The sound of music and singing came clearly to

her through the still evening air as she approached the kraal. She hurried the last few yards and stepped into the cleared circle and looked around. The men were dancing with the chief, while the women and children sat around on the ground, rattling dry seeds in hollow gourds.

The chief stopped the music long enough to give Malla a warm welcome and then went on dancing while Malla watched, wondering where he would let her stay. When the celebration ended, a crowd followed her to a grass-roofed hut, shoving and pushing to be close enough to see her. They broke into excited talk when she unfolded her cot. It was clear they didn't know what it was. When she showed them, by lying down and pretending to be asleep, she could tell their next question was how she kept from falling off in her sleep. Adults and children fingered her toothbrush and comb, passing them from one to another. She had wanted to read to them from the Bible but finally decided all she could do was repeat the few words she had learned from the East Africa Mission people. "God loves all people, white and black."

Not even the noisy night sounds kept her awake. When she opened her eyes the next morning, she saw a ring of black faces watching her from the low open doorway and peering in through chinks they had made in the mud walls. She reached for her Bible before getting up and read John 3:16 slowly and loudly. She determined to use every minute of the month to say something about God whenever she had an audience. And she had a constant audience, with someone always trailing at her heels, eyes curious about everything she did.

The gifts she had brought were an instant attraction, especially the sugar and matches. When the news spread to neighboring kraals that someone had sugar, the chiefs invited Malla to visit their kraals also. Malla knew some of the other missionaries frowned at the idea of giving gifts. "That's just bribery," they insisted.

But Malla shrugged off the ciriticism. "So it is sugar brings them. So they hear God loves them. I show love by gifts."

4

The month in that kraal flew by, and she returned to Emelia and Lizzie long enough to replenish her supplies before setting out for another one. Her mouth was as busy as her hands as she told of her experiences while she packed her equipment.

"I learn so much, Lizzie. First time they offer that dreadful sour milk, my stomach say *no*! One day I so thirsty. I had no water to make tea, so I drink the milk. It terrible! I run behind tree so they not see me throw up. The second and third times just as bad. I don't know if I ever learn to drink it. I know I not ever like it."

"What about sleeping? Did you have any privacy?" Emelia asked.

Malla laughed as she shook her head. "It a good thing it get so dark at night. Someone there every minute around hut, so I wait to undress and go to bed. Even then I not take off many clothes. A head is always sticking in doorway when I open my eyes."

"Did you have a chance to talk to them? To the women at least? And did they understand you?"

Malla's expressive face was sad. "Ah, Lizzie, the poor women. They work so much. There is food to cook, grain to grind, beer to make, so many children— they not have time to sit and listen. And the men!" Her eyes flashed with anger. "The men so busy too—

busy to sit and talk!"

Then her voice softened as she went on. "It is the children and old women who listen. They the only ones with time." She shook her head sorrowfully. "Poor old women—so near end of hard life and no hope of future life. They come. They sit before my hut and listen. I read from Bible. Try to sing—"

She broke off, her eyes filled with tears. "Oh, Lizzie, Emelia! These people so deep in sin. I pray God in His mercy to save dear people. Hearts hard now because crops good. They think king and gods take care of them. All they think of is full stomach with corn and figs and bananas and beer."

"And they are so afraid," Emelia said. "Afraid to die. We had a man come who needed help. He had slashed his skin trying to drive out the evil spirits that were making him sick."

"And he said he was always afraid when he drank beer from his clay pot because some unknown enemy, even one of his own family, might have poisoned it." Lizzie's voice carried her compassion. "Everyone is so bound by fear, either real or imaginary."

Malla was silent for a moment. Then she looked at Lizzie, her voice troubled. "I afraid, too. But we have God. They do not. That is why I go to them. I must be one with them to say they not need to live with fear. God can free them."

"But you must not live by yourself in the kraals for so long a time. A few nights is one thing, but a month—"

Emelia cut into Lizzie's protest with her own. "While you were gone we had word that Mr. Franson has appointed Mr. Dawson to be in charge of our station. And when Mr. Dawson heard what you are doing, he was quite opposed to it. He feels it is dangerous for you. The Africans are always courteous, of course, but he is sure it bothers them to have a white person, and especially a woman alone, living so long with them."

"God bring me here. He take care of me. I must go. I must be one with them. I live with them so they listen." Malla's voice was stubborn as she walked away, her back rigid with determination.

Lizzie looked after her. "She is so stubborn! She will have her way whether it is wise or not. Can't she see how it will set back the work of the whole mission if she gets killed just because she insists on living with the Africans? Living like one of them?"

But Emelia shook her head, her voice coming slowly as she said, "I know she is stubborn. I sometimes want to shake her. She always has an opinion on everything. Yet—there is something different about her. She isn't just a white person going to the kraal to tell ignorant people something she thinks they need."

Emelia stopped, struggling for words. Then she burst out, "Lizzie, I'm ashamed to say this. But I find it hard to sit on the grass mats and sleep in those little mud huts with ants and other vermin—" she stopped, shuddering, and added "—and eat their food, that awful sour milk. Oh, I do it. And so do you. But I don't want to."

Lizzie nodded. "I know what you're saying, and I know it's true. We do all that, but still we remain outsiders. Malla already belongs."

"That's it. She is one of them. I have to remember that when I get so—" She broke off, her face flushed.

Lizzie laughed. "Go ahead and say it. You get angry at her stubbornness and at the gifts she gives so people will sit and listen. I do, too. She thinks she is always right about everything, and there's no changing that. And yet—she does admit when she is wrong—"

"Lizzie, we've known her over a year, and I've never heard her admit any such thing! And what you said about people listening to a Bible story because of getting something. They will agree to anything for a piece of bright colored cloth or a handful of salt. That doesn't mean they understand or believe."

"No, but they do listen. And they don't always listen to me. I have to keep asking God not to let my irritation at Malla and her methods keep me from doing my work."

Emelia sighed. "Yes, she'll do things her way no matter what anyone thinks—"

"If she's convinced God wants her to," Lizzie interrupted. "I have to remember she's stubborn when she thinks she's doing what God wants her to. And now she is planning to go and help in that new station to the north at Hebron. If the woman working there doesn't have help, she will have to close the school."

Emelia laughed. "Malla won't let her close it. She never admits defeat."

But if Lizzie and Emelia had seen Malla later that day, they would have seen her in a time of dark despair. She had gone to spend a few weeks in a kraal before going to Hebron. She had unwittingly reached the kraal in early afternoon, walking in on a beer drink. Only one little girl was sober, and there was no one to show her the hut she was to use. As she sat watching, knowing nothing she did or said would stop the riotous behavior, one drink-crazed African man began to pursue her, trying to kiss her. She was sure that once he caught her he would kill her. No one helped, but instead they laughed and cheered for the man as he ran after Malla. She dodged behind trees, tripping over her long skirts as she tried to stay out of reach of his clutching hands.

Finally, as night came on, people began to settle down. In her hut Malla began to pray out loud. "Who are you talking to?" people called from nearby huts. Malla found it difficult to relax until she remembered the verse "The Lord gives his beloved sleep." Her heart filled with pity as she thought, *These poor people have no one to give them sleep.*

In the morning, many of the people came to express their regret for what had happened the day before, their faces ashamed. The man who had chased her said, "Don't be afraid of me. That was a wild beast, and he has left. Just look at my eyes, and you will see."

By the time she was ready to leave, an old woman, who had sat and listened as Malla told Bible stories in her halting words, said, "I know you are from God. You are not like other white people. You sit with us, you walk with us, you make us happy. You are one of us. Are you going to heaven? I want to be where you are going."

Tears poured down Malla's cheeks as she heard the old woman, knowing she had to leave her and get ready to go to Hebron.

Malla had only planned to stay at Hebron a few weeks to help with the school. But while she was there, the rainy season kept the rivers full and too dangerous to cross. Though she was busy teaching in the school, she decided to visit the kraal of Queen Madolomafish, whom she had heard about from both Africans and missionaries. She went on horseback, taking one of the black people from the station as a helper.

When she got to the kraal, she was taken immediately into the queen's hut, where she had to duck to enter the low doorway. Straightening up and letting her eyes get accustomed to the gloomy interior, she stared at the queen. "She must weigh four hundred pounds!" She was glad no one understood her words, as she watched the queen shovel roasted corn and other food into her mouth. Malla knew the Swazis thought that a fat body was a sign of greatness, but she had never seen anyone so huge.

She managed to turn her astonishment into smiles of sincere greeting. After a brief conversation, she asked, "May I come back for visit? I like to stay in kraal."

"When you come?"

"In one month."

"It is good." The queen nodded.

After praying in a loud voice so that the people crowding around the open doorway could hear, Malla hurried back to Hebron. As she walked briskly, she thought how useless it was to wait a month when she could go back almost at once. Her co-worker advised against it. "You told her a month."

"I get ready now anyhow," Malla answered. She began gathering the supplies she would need and opened her Bible seeking guidance. The pages fell open to Nehemiah 2:8. "The king granted me according to the good hand of my God upon me."

"God wants me to go now," Malla said to her co-worker, and started off in high spirits. But as she went along, doubts crept in. She had said a month, and here it was, only one week later. Maybe she should have listened to advice. Then she shrugged off the doubts and hurried along the dusty trail. Reaching the kraal, she went to the queen's hut. "I come to stay."

"Is that so?" The queen asked the question between enormous mouthfuls of food, her voice unfriendly.

"I may bring in my things?"

The queen ate steadily for several minutes while Malla stood waiting. Finally the queen gave permission, assigning her to a hut with ten young girls who were the king's daughters. The queen's unfriendly reception could have meant danger for Malla. But she was recognized by a woman who had been in a kraal Malla had visited several months earlier. She told the queen how much Malla loved African people and how she gave them gifts. From then on, the queen insisted that Malla share her food and called her "my white child."

But Malla was restless. She had come to make friends, yes. But her burning desire was to open blind eyes to God's love. And every effort she made to talk about God was frustrated by the African habit of changing the subject away from God. At the end of a month, Malla returned to Hebron, feeling there was no more she could do in the queen's kraal.

Her experience there made her realize more than ever how helpless she was in preaching. She needed a helper, an African who knew the language and the people. So she prayed, "God, send young man to be my mouth."

God sent a young Zulu man who had grown up with the fears and superstitions of his tribe. Several times he was almost killed in accidents, which made him wonder what would happen to him after he died. He somehow felt that learning to read would give answers to all his questions and fears. He knew the missionaries could teach him, so he headed for the mission station at Hebron. And he met Malla.

"What you want?" Malla asked.

"I am looking for Jesus." He thought he was saying that he wanted to learn to read, because he didn't know what the name Jesus meant.

Malla took him as God's answer to her prayer. "I

43

still so poor with language, Johane. That is why you go with me to kraals. You tell people message when I not know words."

"But I don't know how to read. I want to learn how."

Malla had to be honest with him. "Johane, I no have home. I live in kraals, staying one month in each. If you come with me, eat what I eat, I teach you to read. Then you preach for me."

Bu Malla's confidence was misplaced. Johane could not learn to read. "Pray God to help you," she urged him repeatedly.

"I have, but it doesn't help. God does not want me to learn."

Malla became as discouraged as Johane and began to wonder if she had been wrong about God's leading. Then one evening he came running to her, his face beaming. Before he could speak, Malla scolded him.

"Where you been? All day I look for you. I have been frightened. I not know what happen to you."

"I can read!"

Malla frowned. "You lying," she said sharply, her worry about him showing itself in anger. "Last night you not read even verses you study all week."

"I can read today. Listen." Johane opened the Bible and read all the pages he had stumbled through so painfully the day before.

"You not really read," Malla scolded. "We have gone many times over those pages. You remember them. You go all day to learn them instead of be here to help."

She snatched the book from him and flipped to the back pages. "You say you know how to read. Read this. This you have not studied."

Johane read the verses without a mistake, with

44

Malla listening, open-mouthed. "You see?" Johane said. "God has taught me to read. I went by myself and cried and prayed and asked God to make me read. He has answered. He said He would teach me. I opened the book, and I knew the words."

He opened the gospel of John to chapter three and read it out loud to the crowd that had come running when they heard his excited voice. Then he said, "I can read this Book now, and it tells me that whoever believes in Jesus Christ, God's Son, will have everlasting life."

Malla listened, tears pouring down her cheeks. Something had happened to Johane. He was a new person. Everyone who heard him read from the Bible and listened to him preach knew that the God in heaven was not just the white man's God. He was not just Malla Moe's God. He was the African boy Johane's God. And He could be their God, too.

"All the power of God. All the grace of God," was Malla's response. She prayed for Johane continually, knowing that heathen culture goes deep and that he faced many pitfalls.

"Johane is heavy on my heart," she wrote in her diary. "Oh, that he not be misfit in the faith. May he be useful to God's glory among own people."

And Johane prayed, "God, go with me and protect me, that I may do Your work and be watchful like my teacher, Miss Moe, has told me to be."

5

Johane spent every spare minute reading the Zulu Bible. He wanted his own people to know about God, so Malla and Lizzie went with him and helped him give reading lessons from Zulu language charts.

After several days of teaching, Johane said, "My chief, the great Maja, lives twenty-five miles from here. Perhaps he will listen when I read from the Book—and let his people listen."

"Chief Maja!" Malla exclaimed. "Oh, I heard of him. I am praying for a way to reach him. I go with you."

"It is a long way to the kraal. The paths are rough, and we must walk," Johane warned.

"That is nothing when someone is there who must hear about God," Malla replied, brushing off Johane's worries. But by the end of the first day, the stony paths hurt Malla's feet so badly that they were swollen and very painful. Johane had to carry her part of the way, especially across the stony river bottoms. But both were so eager to get to the chief that they kept on.

In fact, Malla was so eager to meet this great chief that she ignored all she had learned in the three years she had been in Africa. When they reached his kraal, Malla didn't wait meekly at the edge of the clearing until the chief recognized her presence and accepted the gifts she brought. Instead, she walked boldly into the middle of the circled huts.

"Where is Maja?" she demanded loudly.

The sight and sound of a white woman striding into the kraal without asking the chief's permission brought everything in the village to a dead stop. All sound—the women's chattering, the squeals of children chasing one another around the huts, even the animal noises—seemed cut off in mid air.

Johane trembled as he saw the scowl on Chief Maja's face. "Teacher," he whispered in a shaking voice. "Come back. You must wait."

He stood some distance away from Malla and listened as the chief turned to one of his counselors. "Who is this person? Where is she from?"

Malla understood the chief's questions and answered them herself. "Chief Maja, I come preach to you."

Johane knew he had to step forward now and try to deflect the chief's anger. When Maja thundered again, "Who is she?" Johane answered, "She is a princess."

"What does she want?"

"She wants to talk about the Great One."

The chief's scowl became less threatening. "You mean Queen Victoria?" He nodded approvingly. "It is natural that a white woman would talk about the great white queen."

"No," Johane answered. "She came to talk about the Great One in heaven." He still watched the chief uneasily and felt his shoulders slump in relief when Maja's heavy frown disappeared completely.

Johane still was not sure what reception they would receive in the morning when the chief called for them. But after listening to Malla's words as Johane translated them, Maja nodded approvingly again.

"I have had many dealings with white people. I have found them tricky. They cheat us, thinking we are ignorant. But you, white woman, I see love in you. Come. I have white man's food. You will eat."

Malla shook her head. "Maja, we not come to eat food. We want to teach children. We need place for school."

The next day the chief showed them a place they could use. He watched Malla and Johane kneel and thank God, dedicating the land to His service. Then they hurried back to their station with the good news. Everyone pitched in to gather materials to build a new station, with the school as the center. They arranged for a wagon to take them and their supplies to Maja's kraal.

In three weeks Malla, Johane, and Mr. and Mrs. Dawson and their baby headed eagerly back to the kraal. They decided to leave the wagonload of supplies at the foot of the mountain until they were again sure of Maja's welcome. As they approached the kraal on foot, Johane stopped, his head cocked as he listened intently.

"What is the matter?" Mr. Dawson asked.

Johane shook his head. "I don't know. But look." He pointed to the kraal as they came from the shelter of the trees to the clearing. They saw men sharpening spears and battle axes and making shields. Women scurried about cooking great quantities of food and storing it in a huge cave in the mountainside near the kraal. Even the children were working instead of playing.

When the chief saw the missionaries, he scowled at them. "No, you cannot be here. We prepare for war. The new king in Swaziland thinks he will defeat us. We show him that he cannot. So you cannot stay. It

49

is dangerous for you. Go away. Maybe you come another time."

Malla tried arguing with him, but it did no good. She could not so easily give up her dream of establishing her first mission station and having a school. But they could do nothing but trudge back down the mountainside, wondering if they were mistaken about God's leading.

Malla looked at the wagon loaded with building materials, ready to be used. What should they do now? Emma Dawson fixed the evening meal, urging Malla to eat. "You'll feel better." But Malla was sure she wouldn't.

"We'll camp here for the night," Mr. Dawson decided. "Then tomorrow we'll have to return to Bulunga station. The wagon driver is eager to be on his way. Perhaps God will open something for us later."

Malla took her plate and sat down on the ground, her back against a tree. Her mind kept asking, *God, why this happen? These people need school.* At the sound of footsteps she looked up and saw an African running along the path. Mr. Dawson took the note he carried, read it, and exclaimed, "Listen to this. It is from a chief in a nearby kraal, who wants a lady missionary to come and teach the children."

Malla jumped up. "Oh, that is for me. I know that chief. He and I shared same hut one afternoon from bad thunderstorm. I go."

Mr. Dawson looked at his wife and shrugged his shoulders. It was no use discussing the move with Malla when her mind was made up. And, anyway, it did seem like an answer to prayer. The next day they moved the building materials to the new site and unloaded them.

"I don't like to leave you without helping you put

up a house." Mr. Dawson's concern showed on his face.

"You go," Malla insisted. "If wagon go without you, it is long walk back to station for Emma and the little one. We build."

Johane looked at the pile of supplies. "Can we build a house?"

"God will help us," Malla answered. She had Johane clear the land and begin the walls. They built a little two-room structure, one side for Malla and the other for Johane. Her side was roofed with tin, his with thatch, and both leaked terribly in the heavy rain.

But Malla was happy. It was her home, the first she had had since coming to Africa. She soon had five boys and two girls as pupils. She fretted because the school was so small and, as usual, did something about it. If children from other kraals would not come to her, she would go to them. So she and Johane took their pupils along when they went on preaching trips.

Malla was delighted at the evidence of Johane's spiritual gifts. People listened to him and were saved as he preached the Word. But as the months passed, famine began to creep over the land, hitting their area too. Whenever they went to a kraal, they took their own food along so they would not eat the meager rice and sour milk the villagers offered out of politeness.

Hordes of grasshoppers had eaten the crops, leaving the fields bare and parched. Entire kraals were deserted because the men sent their wives and children back to the wives' parents to live while they roamed the countryside searching for food.

Malla kept reassuring Johane. "He who sends grasshoppers knows our needs. We face hunger, but we not die. The harder it get, the more we give praise to God when He deliver."

"But, teacher, we have only enough rice for one meal. God has forgotten us," Johane blurted.

"No, no, Johane. We like widow in Bible who say she cook what little she had and then die. But God sent enough—more than enough. We like that. We shall receive," Malla said confidently. She went on with what she was doing while Johane stood watching, twisting a stick in his hand.

"But I cannot stay," he finally said. "I have heard that my mother is in great need. And my sister. They are starving. I must go to them. I must help. I must get a job in Johannesburg."

"Johane! You not leave God's work for job. Trust God. He supply for your mother and for us."

"My mother needs me. I must go," Johane repeated, his voice and face stubborn.

The next day Malla watched his thin figure, shoulders bowed, disappear along the path until it was hidden by the trees. Discouragement overwhelmed her. She was sure she could hear Satan whispering, *Why don't you go home. You can't expect anything from these Africans. Why waste your time on them?*

No, said another voice. She knew it was God speaking in her mind, because she had heard His voice many times. *Remember, "He who conquers his own spirit is better than he who takes a city."*

"I will stay," she said out loud. "I not alone because God is with me."

But it was lonely living by herself in the little house she and Johane had built. The children were no longer coming to school. Some had moved away, while others were too weak or sick to come. So Malla moved into a little deserted, broken-down hut near the home of Mr. Henwood, a white man who had married an African woman. The hut had only one tiny, gloomy room. The small entrance had no door to close out the night, but at least that allowed a trickle of daylight to enter the room. She began the school again, bribing children to come by offering prizes. She wrote Johane regularly, not really expecting she would ever see him again. Then one day, three months later, he walked up to the hut, calling Malla's name bashfully.

"My job did not give me enough money to help my mother," he admitted, "so I have come back." Then he looked at the little hut, stooping to peer inside. "You wrote me that you lived in a house," he said accusingly. "But this—this—" He gestured at the crumbling walls. The loose sheets of metal that formed the roof had to be held in place by heavy stones. "You are like an ant crawling in and out!"

Malla shrugged off his pity impatiently. "But now you have returned. God has brought you back. The famine still bad, but God will supply. He gives all we need, not all we want. There is much work for God to do in this place."

With the coming of the rainy season, the danger from the famine lessened. Malla was able to buy several cows so they would not be dependent on others for milk. She and Johane worked tirelessly, planting potatoes and corn. The memory of the many hungry days they had lived through drove them to work even in the hot noon sun.

They stayed in the little hut for a year and a half, happy because of the many who came to listen to Johane preach. People sat in the dirt, crowding around the hut and holding branches over their heads to keep off the sun. They listened to Johane in amazement.

"You are so young, and yet you know so much. Has this white woman taught you all this?"

"Yes, I have learned much from the missionary. But it is when Jesus comes into the heart that you learn. He teaches the secret things from His Book."

Johane also taught Malla many ways to win the confidence of the people. "You must always have food on hand. And everyone must feel welcome to stop and share it."

"But if there is not enough?" Malla asked.

"They will know there is not much. They will take only a small mouthful. They know how to share."

People in surrounding kraals soon knew that a white missionary lived near them whose home was always open to them and who always fed them. Her home was just like theirs, so they did not feel shy with her. When they came for a meal, they found that she had very little physical food, but she fed them spiritually.

Malla was happy that at last she was learning to make the clicks of the Zulu language. By making herself speak it exclusively, she was beginning to be accurate and could be understood. "I want so much to be one with these dear black people," she said over and over again.

When other missionaries visited her station, they heard the African women explaining why they felt so free with Malla. "She sits with us on the floor of our huts, she eats our food and shares hers with us, she knows our names, she never forgets us."

In spite of this, Malla was sad. She had lived in the little hut for a year and a half, and not one person had asked Jesus to be his Savior. She visited the kraals, walking for miles in the blistering sun. She squatted with the Africans in their huts, swatting flies. People listened. They asked questions and talked

54

about the gospel, but not one would accept it. They simply shook their heads with a polite smile and shrug of their shoulders.

Again, discouragement was a mountain she could not see over. Three times as she set out to visit kraals she imagined she could hear Satan sneering, *You'll never see a Swazi converted. You had better go home and rest.*

But that third time she met a blind boy and invited him to the meetings in her house. He came, listened intently, accepted Jesus, and wanted to go at once and preach to his people. Malla named him Barnabas. "Johane! Our very first convert. You see? The devil a liar. The very day he say no Swazi be converted, God give us this boy."

The conversion of Barnabas was a breakthrough in the work Malla and Johane did in the kraals. Her visits had taught her many things which she passed on to other missionaries who did not live in the kraals for months at a time as she did.

"We not need to be good preachers to be good missionaries. When Africans saved they make good preachers. They preach better than we can. We need just to show how to live after salvation. They must know what it mean to sacrifice for Jesus."

Some of the missionaries resented Malla's dictatorial ways, but they could not argue with her example. She lived her own advice, going to the kraals with the simplest of provisions and becoming one with the people.

Because she lived with them, she knew how hard it was for some of the converts to change their life-style immediately. She strongly believed that accepting Christ meant a changed life. She also believed she should not lecture but should let the Holy Spirit do His work.

55

One group of believers kept their previous habit of drinking beer at parties, sometimes leading to drunkenness. Malla and Johane suggested to the group that they set aside one whole day to pray definitely about the situation. As a result, all but one family agreed that, because they were Christians, they should no longer drink beer. "Beer drinking does not match our new faith," the leader said.

The family who insisted on drinking protested. "We are old Christians. You were just born yesterday. Who are you to tell us what we should do?"

The new believers answered, "We do not teach you. We look to God's Word to teach us and you."

Some of Malla's fellow missionaries chided her. "You are not wise to leave the solution of such an important matter to converts who are less than a year old in the faith."

"But I not always be there to settle problems," Malla answered. "I have give the Word of God. I teach them fast and pray about problems. When they do, God give them answers better than mine."

God also gave Malla an answer to her desperate housing need. She was offered land for a house so she could move out of the decrepit sod building. Johane had to be the builder, and he prayed out loud as he placed each stone in place. "I am not a builder," he explained. "God must tell me what to do so the house will not fall down when I am through."

Even though the house was small, it had two rooms, one for Malla and the girls to sleep in, the other for Johane and the boy students.

"At last I have a home!" Malla exclaimed, walking around it and clapping her hands. "I have been here four years and have no place called home. I name it Bethel because it not my house. It is God's house."

The classes for the students were held outside

except in rainy weather. The children found that Malla was more than a teacher. Most of them came to school with only the clothes on their backs. Malla not only provided their food, but she made them clothes when the old ones wore out. Since she had no patterns to follow, she invented a simple system. She just spread the materials on the floor, laid the boy or girl on top, and cut around the figure for the proper size. Then she sewed up the side seams to make the knee-length shirts for the boys and kimono-like dresses for the girls.

Malla was happier than she had ever been. She had a house to live in, children to teach, a garden to care for, and people to witness to. She wrote in her diary. "O God, you have made me so glad it cannot be told."

Her main thought was that people must be saved. She remembered how unhappy she had been before she accepted Jesus, and she knew He had changed her life. "Are you saved?" she asked everyone she met. "You must be saved—not to be lost."

By now her letters home began to report, "Some are saved almost every meeting. All grace of God."

6

But along with the happiness Malla felt because of all that was happening in the work, she was worried as rumors spread that war was coming to the land.

"What is this trouble that comes to our country?" Africans kept asking her.

She tried to explain as clearly as she could, even though she didn't understand all the rumors herself. "It is trouble between our Dutch friends, the Boers, and the British people who work in the gold mines at Johannesburg and other places. Each side wants to say to others what to do and what to think."

"But we are not Dutch or British," Johane protested. "We are Zulus and Swazis. It does not concern us, this quarrel between British and Dutch."

"But both sides want missionaries to be for them," Malla answered. "We cannot do that. We have friends on both sides."

Malla was deeply troubled about their Dutch neighbors. Many of them had a strong religious background but did not have a life-changing Christian faith. They looked down on the Africans, treating them as inferior. Malla more than once had stomped off in anger from a Boer neighbor after a discussion about whether Africans had souls. If war did come, she knew many of her Boer neighbors would die. She knew she had not witnessed to them as she had to the Africans.

When it was certain that war would break out at any moment, Mr. Dawson tried to persuade Malla to leave Bethel for a safer station.

"We not in danger here," she insisted. She refused to go to the Bulunga station where the other missionaries were. "If war come, then maybe I go. Maybe."

Mr. Dawson had to be satisfied with that almost-promise.

War did break out in October 1899, and all white people were told they must leave Swaziland. The missionaries at Bulunga made plans to move to a station near the coast to wait out the war, which they thought would be brief. Mr. Dawson sent a runner to Bethel to tell Malla to meet them in three days at a place near her station. The rest of the missionary group reached the point of rendezvous and waited for Malla to come.

Several days passed with no sign of her. Finally Emma Dawson said, "As usual, Malla has decided to do what she wants to regardless of other people's plans. I did not think she would come."

"I'm sure she didn't want to give the people the idea that she was running from danger—"

"Neither did we, Lizzie," Emma replied. "You've worked with Malla long enough to know that she can't stand being dictated to, even when it's for her own safety."

"Well, I regret leaving her, but we've waited three days. She would have had time to meet us if she wanted to. We'll have to go on," Mr. Dawson reluctantly decided. "She is safe as far as the Africans are concerned. They love her and would not harm her. We'll need to ask God to keep her safe from the soldiers."

Malla's missionary friends would have prayed even

harder for her if they had known that the messenger had never reached her. She did not know of the plans to leave, did not know of the other missionaries' anxious wait for her, and did not know that she was left as the lone white person in Swaziland.

Her friends did not worry about her safety, because the stories about the war that trickled in to them were incomplete. They did not think she was in any danger. Actually, soldiers for the Boer side swarmed over Swaziland, taking food, cattle, and anything else they wanted. The soldiers were dangerous if they were drunk.

Malla and Johane and the children were in constant danger, because soldiers were always present, patrolling the roads. If the patrols were friendly when they stopped at Bethel for food, they often listened to Malla talk to them about Christ. Other patrols threatened her, demanding to know why she, a single white woman, lived with Africans. Since some Africans looted Dutch homes whose men were away fighting, the Dutch soldiers didn't like anyone who liked Africans. And Malla obviously liked Africans.

The news spread that a white woman missionary still remained in Swaziland. Along with the news went the rumor that Malla was a spy for the British. They claimed that the many letters she wrote contained information about Boer troop movements.

Someone complained, "That white woman purposely stayed where she is in order to listen and report to the British what we are doing. She sends information in her letters."

The commander of the Boer forces ordered Malla to answer the charges.

"No, no," she protested. "I write letter to encourage Africans who so afraid. I have met many in distant kraals. I cannot travel now to see them. By letter I remind them about God. See?" She held out a letter she had just written. "I do what Paul in Bible do. He could not visit converts, so he write them. I do that too."

Her sincerity convinced the commander. But he ordered, "Do not send the letters anymore by special runner. Use the regular mail."

"That too slow," she protested. "Letters must go fast in order to help."

Since she kept writing as many letters as before and sending them by every means possible, complaints kept pouring in that she was a threat to Boer army security. Somehow she must be forced to leave.

When the army officer came with the order that she was to join the other white people near the coast, he found Malla suffering from painful, swollen eyes.

"What happened to you?" he asked, his voice suspicious.

"My coffee slow to boil. I try to hurry it. I blow into spout, and hot coffee grounds fly in eyes. It due to my old impatience," she admitted candidly.

If she expected sympathy from the soldiers, she was disappointed. They gave her the brusque order to pack up and leave. "Two days from now you must be on your way."

"But I have no wagon to go so far."

"You have a small cart."

"But it have no cover. It cold and rainy weather, and I not a well person."

"We'll make you a covering." As Malla watched helplessly, the two soldiers cut sticks and then used one of her blankets to make a simple covering. They let four of her African helpers go with her for protection on the road.

"Where we to go?" she asked.

"Anywhere, as long as you leave Swaziland," the soldiers answered.

African believers from the surrounding kraals followed the little bedraggled procession as it wound along the narrow trail. Their mother was being taken from them, and they were sure they would never see her again.

Even Malla did not see how God could work in this situation. She was discouraged because of the pain of her sore eyes and the pain of leaving her dear people at Bethel. Even though she was able to have services in kraals she visited during her exile, she was terribly discouraged. Visiting a kraal one day when the people were preparing for a heathen celebration, she felt so dry and useless that she just shrugged her shoulders and walked away without trying to talk to them about Jesus.

Finally, after many weeks, she sent one of her boys to the Boer commander asking that he allow her to return to Bethel. She could hardly believe it when he sent word that she could return for a visit.

When her cart pulled into the clearing of the Bethel station, people heard the creaking wheels and came running, shouting, "It is the missionary! It is Malla Moe!" They crowded into the church with her and listened as she thanked God for His goodness. "Now, God, You see I back. We know nothing about the future, God. But, God, You know."

The Boer soldiers watched Malla closely for the next several weeks. Finally the commander gave her permission to stay at Bethel. "But you must not travel out to distant kraals, and you must not write so many letters."

Malla went her usual way, ignoring the travel restrictions whenever she saw a need in some kraal. As the war went on for many long months, people came to ask her for help with their spiritual needs as well as their physical needs.

God used Malla and Johane in ordinary ways, but He also worked for them in special needs, sometimes showing His power in miracles. During 1901 a serious drought hit Swaziland. Many Africans who were not believers blamed Malla for the lack of rain.

"It's because of that white woman's presence. The spirits are angry that she did not leave with the other white people. The spirits do not want the white people here. If she left, the queen could order rain to come."

Johane could not let that challenge pass. He called the believers together to pray for rain. "God answered Elijah when he prayed for rain. He will answer our prayer too."

After a time of earnest praying, the believers and those who had come to mock the Christians began to move toward their homes. As they went, dark clouds rolled over the skies. Before they could reach their huts, the heavy rain poured down. When the storm was over and people looked around, they could see that it was not an accidental happening. A heavy hail had come with the rain and had badly damaged the crops of those who had spoken against Malla. But the believers' crops were standing green under a gentle rain.

The year 1901 brought war even closer to the Bethel station. Every day people watched and listened to the troops marching along the road. At first there were Boer soldiers fleeing in disorganized panic from British forces. Whenever they stopped at the station, Malla bandaged their wounds and gave food and drink and a chance to rest. She and Johane and their helpers always talked to the soldiers about God and His love. Because of the soldiers' fears and misery, they were willing to listen.

"He's the only One who can help us now," one of the soldiers responded.

Malla knew they were thinking only about victory in war and she shook her head vigorously. "No, no! You need His help for you. Long after war is over, you will have peace in heart if you ask for it now."

Most of the soldiers just shook their heads at her invitation and pressed on, waiting for a chance to strike back at the enemy.

Then one day three thousand British troops poured into Swaziland, passing Bethel to camp a few miles down the road. Those at the station watched for four hours as the soldiers marched by, some swinging along in step, others on horseback.

Some of the African helpers peered out of doorways, shivering as they watched. "They bring more trouble for us," they said sadly. "Soldiers always take what they want of our belongings. If we do not give willingly, they take anyway and kill us if they want to."

"Maybe these soldiers will be different," someone suggested, but no on believed it.

Then Malla discovered that the commander of the British troops, General Edmund H. Allenby, had given his soldiers strict orders. They were to buy what they needed, paying the people a good price, and they were not to molest the Africans in any way.

General Allenby heard about the rich crop of sweet potatoes at the Bethel station and sent soldiers to buy a large supply. Malla's quick mind seized the opportunity to be friends with such an important person.

"I will make a cake for this big person," she told Johane. She sent an invitation to Allenby to visit her for dinner and bring some of his officers.

General Allenby had heard about this lone white woman who was isolated in the hills of Swaziland by choice. She was the only white person who had stayed, other than the Boers who lived in Swaziland. When he visited, the general discovered that she had stayed because of her desire to reach Africans for Christ.

Malla soon discovered that she and the general shared a mutual faith in Christ. They had many talks about God during the ten days he was stationed with his troops near Bethel. Allenby told her that he was trying to give the Boers a chance to surrender without a battle and so save lives. When he was unsuccessful, he and his troops moved on.

Malla and her helpers felt that Allenby's soldiers had been "God's angels" to them by getting them supplies of food and clothing they desperately needed. When the British soldiers left, the Boers returned, once again taking what crops and other supplies they wanted without paying for them.

The return of problems, and Malla's inability to feel the compassion for the Boer soldiers that she had for the British, brought back a flood of discouragement. Malla's personality could plunge her from heights of happiness to deepest gloom.

When she was happy, her favorite expression was "Ooooh, I jump when I so happy at what God can do." She wrote in her diary many times, "Joy and sorrow travel together."

Her emotional life was affected by what happened to her, to her friends, to casual acquaintances, and even to people who did not like her. She even grieved for the wives a man gave up when he became a Christian. She was often depressed by the needs of other people, especially those who were sick and hungry. The war years were hard on everyone, since food supplies were cut off and what food they could grow was taken by the soldiers. Along with the dangers of war, they faced the constant threat of drought or hail or grasshoppers, which would destroy the corn or sweet potato crop.

One morning Malla wrote in her diary, "Since Sunday I have not felt God in my heart. I have not felt Him among my children. Last night I was surprised and could not sleep for fear. I felt empty and dry, so I thought I sinned against Holy Spirit. I prayed the Lord's prayer three times and after went to sleep. This morning I woke with same feeling. I found the promise in Revelation 2:2-6. I read to all of them, explained my feelings, and asked if it true we do not have our 'first love.' Joseph sang song Johane had written. 'In heaven no sin shall come in, hallelujah, hallelujah.' Joseph sang and cried, and I cry, too. We cried all of us, and we again prayed, all of us. After that I feel God's Spirit near us, and tonight it is good again. Now I am happy again. Praise the Lord for His mercy and grace."

The end of the Boer War in May 1902 brought some release from the fear and tension people had lived under for more than two years. But it did not erase the hatred from people's hearts. Thousands of homeless, frantic Dutch farmers streamed past Bethel for many months after the peace treaty was signed. Malla urged them to stop, and those who did were given food and drink and were offered the water of salvation.

The end of the war lifted the restrictions on travel, so Malla and Johane were able to get back into the hills to visit the kraals and renew friendships. Malla also began to plan for a longer trip.

"I have been here ten years," she told Johane. "It time to go to America. I must see how my family live."

"How soon will you go?"

"I wait until Mr. Dawson comes to take my place here. He has big job now to tour all mission stations to see that everything is running good. The station at Bulunga was broken down and looted by soldiers and people. Termites eat station where Emelia Forbord is. Mr. Dawson must see to new buildings. When he comes back, I go."

Johane hated to see Malla leave and was pleased that it took Mr. Dawson longer than he expected to return to Bethel with his family. Malla was not free to leave for America until July 1903.

7

As soon as news spread that she was going away, people crowded around asking, "Malla, are you really leaving us?"

"No, no, I not leave. I just go for visit. I come back."

"But what will we do without you? How can we believe unless you are here?"

"You can believe to Mr. Dawson," Malla answered the women. "He will tell you same that I would."

One woman shook her head. "No, it is you I want to believe to. It was from you I first heard the gospel." Nothing Malla said could change her mind.

Malla found herself in tears as she packed to leave. Christians from distant kraals crowded in to Bethel for a farewell service. The people insisted over and over again that if she went, she would never return.

"How can I go?" Malla asked fellow missionaries.

Mr. Dawson felt himself torn between both sides and began to wonder if he would be able to step into this work where Malla was so dearly loved.

Finally one of the African believers gently scolded the people. "You are not doing right to weep like this. We all know it is God's will for Malla Moe to go home after ten years in Swaziland. She has people in America she loves. She wants to visit them and tell them about us. Do not make her heart sad. God has given us Mr. Dawson to help us until she returns. God wants her to see her people once again."

Though his words helped ease the emotional tension, no one was willing to go to his own home on the last day she was in Bethel. "We are here to look after you. This is the last day. We could not be anywhere else. We have to be where you are. You are our heart."

Almost everyone went part of the way with her, running along the path behind the wagon in which she rode. Johane and some of the close African helpers accompanied her to Durban for the final, sad parting. They remained there for two weeks until the ship was ready to sail. Finally on July 27, 1903, the big ship slid out of the harbor into the waters for the long journey to America.

"I cannot yet say I go home," Malla brooded as she stood on deck. "Home is my dear people in Swaziland."

She waved back to Emelia and the others standing on the pier, her heart lifted as always in prayer. "God, bless your work. Use and bless all white workers who come out. So many come now. Reveal yourself to Africans. Unite us in your love. Be glorified in me while I home. May I feel always poor in spirit, needing you."

Malla paced the deck of the ship during the weeks of travel. She had been used to walking miles every week and found it impossible to sit. She wished she had kept track of the thousands of miles she had walked in the past ten years over narrow, stony paths, often cutting through underbrush and wading across rivers. Her mission in life was to bring the gospel of life in Christ to people who didn't know Him, and so she had walked those miles carrying that message. She was temporarily leaving that mission field. Now, here on this ship, was another opportunity to be a witness for Christ. That was her life no matter where she was.

The weather was stormy the week it took to sail from Durban to Capetown. Huge waves and strong winds battered the ship constantly, causing adults as well as children to scream from fear. Malla was almost glad for this, because she was sure their fright would make people think more seriously about God. But when she went to the Sunday morning service, she found hardly anyone there.

"Why more people not come to service?" she asked one of the ship's officers.

He shrugged. "Why should they bother? The minister doesn't preach anything worth listening to. Anyway, he doesn't live any differently through the week than they do."

Malla tried to talk to people about Christ, but no one was interested. "I have not found one Christian," she wrote in her diary. "Oh, to talk to my dear black believers."

Several young men watched her, laughing together at her broken English and her old-fashioned clothes. One of them strolled over to her one day as she stood at the railing, her thoughts back with her dear friends at Bethel.

"I have a very important question to ask you." He winked at two of his friends, who had moved closer, expecting to have some fun with this peculiar person. "The Bible has been translated so many times, we can't possibly believe it, can we?"

"You not know that those who study Hebrew and Greek find most translations true?" Her surprise at his ignorance was so clear that the young man became angry.

His voice was harsh as he said, "Missionaries are the worst people that have ever come to South Africa. They are ruining the people. Africans who go to the mission stations for learning no longer want to work."

Someone standing in the crowd that had gathered to listen said, "Besides, missionaries always try to change the customs of the people. They are happy as they are, with their own way of doing things, with their own gods."

"Yah." Malla nodded, her voice heavy with sadness. "I have seen that happiness you talk about. It is not good. The people live always with fear of evil spirit. They believe the black magic of the witch doctor. I live in their huts. I see this."

"You have actually stayed in their villages? Lived with them? You, a white person?"

Malla looked at the woman who asked the question and tried to explain that it was a person's relationship to God that was important, not his race or education or wealth.

"Do you mean that if you had the choice between staying with a believing African and an unbelieving white person, you would choose the African?"

"Yah. I am most at home with believing Africans."

"As a white person, you should be ashamed of yourself," the woman responded angrily and turned away, her contempt for Malla showing clearly on her face.

A man who had stood on the fringe of the group moved closer to Malla as she stood by the railing. He saw the tears on her cheeks and said, "Don't mind these people. That young man who started the conversation is an English lord. He not only thinks he is better than blacks, he thinks he is better than most whites, too."

"He does not know how people change when they believe Jesus. I know. I have seen."

The man smoked in silence for a few moments, and then he said, "A lot of these people say they are Christians, but they don't talk about it. At least, not on board ship. I've seen a lot of people like that. That's why I never had paid any attention to Christianity. I have always thought that if it was something to be ashamed of, then it wasn't worth believing."

"It not like that," Malla replied eagerly, glad for this first real opportunity on board ship to reach someone for Christ.

The man stared out across the long reaches of blue water and listened as Malla explained how the Lord Jesus had come to die for his sins and give him eternal life. He took his cigar out of his mouth and glanced at her, his eyes surveying her old-fashioned black dress and unbecoming hat.

A faint smile touched his face as he said, "I've never met a person like you. You seem to be a full-time Christian outside of church as well as inside."

"You can be, too," Malla urged. "Just believe. Just say yes to Jesus. That work for white person as well as black. It worked for me."

He smiled, tipped his hat, and turned away. Malla watched him stroll along the deck and felt the tears come again. "God, you know he needs you. Save him like You do my Africans."

She prayed hard for the people on the ship during the rest of the voyage and couldn't help wondering if she would find this same attitude among people in America. Would there be people who were Christians in church but not outside it?

When she arrived in Chicago in September, her family welcomed her warmly. But Malla was brokenhearted to find that Dorothea had no interest in spiritual things. She had a good teaching position and many friends, but she had no interest in church. And Malla blamed herself, wondering if her leaving Dorothea had made her forever bitter toward God.

Fortunately, though she prayed for her sister harder than ever, Malla had no time to brood and become depressed. She was swept into traveling and speaking before church groups, who were eager to hear of all that had happened during her ten years in Africa. People listened intently as she told of the mighty things God had done.

"It was God did it, not me," she insistently explained. "I just poor, uneducated farm girl. God healed through me because I know nothing of medicine. God bring crops because I not a farmer. God built buildings because I know nothing of construction. God feed and clothe people because I have no money. Because I a lone woman, it is God who did it all."

Everywhere she went, she told of the tremendous needs of the struggling churches she had left in South Africa. "We need new missionaries. Not enough now to go around everywhere there is need," she pleaded. She talked often to people about Johane and read to her audiences the letters she received from him.

"My dear mother in Christ," he wrote, "the one who gave me birth in the gospel, Miss Malla Moe. God's peace from our Lord Jesus be with you. The work here at Bethel seems very heavy now. I fasted three days and prayed. After that we had a good meeting. It did my heart good to hear the Christians pray and testify. We are going to have a special meeting to pray for you."

In another letter he said, "It hurts me to see that

Mr. Dawson has so much work to do. He has preaching trips, government and tribal contacts to make, looking after the new churches, seeing about the schools for children, helping the other missionaries. He also has to do the women's work of sewing clothes for the young converts. Another thing worries me, Mother. It is that the Christians will have to scatter because of the famine that is so bad. Can you get some help for us?"

"What causes so many famines over there?" someone asked Malla after one meeting.

"We so often have plague of grasshoppers. They swoop down and eat all that is green to bare, brown earth. Many animal diseases kill cattle. Poeple have nothing to eat."

None of Malla's explanations conveyed the terrible need as clearly as Johane's simple words. "We forget about our hunger when we are in the meetings. But when we go out among the people, we remember as we see their need. They have nothing. Many people have no clothes and must go only in a loincloth. They go many days without food. Here at Bethel we have it good, as we can get one meal a day."

Malla not only read Johane's letters to church groups but had them published in church papers and magazines in order to reach as many people as possible. The letters always brought responses both in money and in increased interest and prayer for the work.

Malla was bold in her appeals for help, making clear that she was not asking for money for herself but for the people and work God had called her to. She wrote for one magazine, "The work of the Lord has been put in the hands of His children. If there is lack of funds, it must be that they are not doing what they ought to do, and what He has told them to do. We are told not to gather treasures here on earth."

Money came in for the work not only because of Johane's letters, but also because of what Mr. Dawson wrote to mission headquarters. He was amazed at the work Malla had done. "I had no idea how sacrificially she lived or how extensively she traveled. She never thought of her money, meager as it was, as *her* money, but put it back into the work. Her example has caused the African believers to live as she does."

Much of the money was given to her directly, and she was able to forward money to the field frequently. Johane's letters told her of specific needs, and she sent money for them.

Malla could also tell people in America how unselfish her African workers were. One church where she spoke was so impressed by Johane that it sent a special personal Christmas gift to him. His reply came quickly.

"Please thank all the givers for me. But also kindly tell them that the money was used for something else. I trust this will not cause misunderstanding. There were seventeen new converts that needed clothing. The money was used for that. My wish is that your crowns will be much brighter than ours, because it is you who are doing the work out here."

Malla eagerly read each of Johane's letters and could tell that he was growing in his Christian experience. She knew how much he had depended on her as the one who had brought him to the Lord. She had been afraid that his faith was in *her* faith rather than in God.

Now he wrote about how much Mr. Dawson's leadership was helping him grow stronger in his

Christian life. He wrote about how quickly Mr. Dawson had mastered the Zulu language and how he was organizing a committee to put hymns into the Zulu language and was teaching the people to sing. Malla smiled as she read that and blinked away tears of homesickness. It would be so good to be back at Bethel and hear the beautiful way Mr. Dawson could sing.

Then Johane wrote about Mr. Franson's visit to South Africa and to Swaziland. Malla couldn't help a feeling of jealousy and regret that she had not been at Bethel to welcome the man who had sent her to Africa.

"Ah, how he preaches," Johane wrote. "He knows how to use the illustrations we so love."

Malla knew that Mr. Franson did not find a great mass of people who had been saved in South Africa in the years she and the others had lived there. But the ones who were believers were genuine believers. And during 1906 while Mr. Franson was there, a revival took place, and many were saved.

Johane wrote of what God had done for him through Mr. Franson's preaching. He came into a relationship with Christ that he hadn't known before.

"My spirit seems to be cleansed, and all the gifts which I seemed to have had before have disappeared. All I am left with is my faith in Christ. Now I walk with Him. When I sleep, when I wake, when I work, I rejoice in Christ. The things that worried me so much before have been taken away."

Malla, too, needed the teaching from God's Word that she found in America. She had felt like a runner at the end of a long race who needed a long, cold drink of water. She had preached so much in Africa. Now she needed to sit still and listen.

She also eagerly looked forward to the one year of

her three-year furlough that she planned to spend in Norway. Often in Africa, trudging along the narrow paths under the blazing sun, she had longed for the cool mountain air in Norway. She wanted to visit family and friends and relive the experiences of the past. But she also wanted to be a witness for Christ and let relatives and friends know that they could have the joy that she had.

But the year there was a series of bitter disappointments. Most of the ministers of Norwegian churches would not let her speak to their people. One reason they opposed her was that she was a woman. Another was that she had not been sent out as a missionary by the State church. And they were not used to her abrupt way of talking to people about their need of salvation. "Your tactics may work in Africa, but not in Norway," one minister told her.

Malla was able to hold small Bible study groups that met outside the church. Some people who came did not like her critical attitude toward Norwegian ministers and did not feel comfortable with her abrupt manner. Yet they could see that she loved God and loved people.

She went back to America to plan for her return to Swaziland, eager to get back to those who were dearer to her than her own family. She headed back to her beloved believers with money pledged for her work far beyond her dreams and leaving behind many new prayer helpers. And she took with her two new missionaries, Gina Knudsen and Mina Madsen.

8

Malla used the two-month trip from New York to Capetown to witness to everyone she could. Life on the ship was as she remembered it from the trip home three years before. Her heart ached for the people who knew nothing about God and who didn't want to know Him.

But she also filled Gina and Mina with as much knowledge as possible about South Africa to prepare them for the new experiences that waited for them. She described life in the kraals, telling of the dirt and animals and sour milk. She talked about the people's warmth and courtesy and friendliness. But most of all she described their spiritual need and hunger.

The three women changed ships at Capetown for Durban, and from there they took a train to a town more than two hundred miles north.

"How do we go from there?" Gina asked.

"God always provide a way," Malla answered. "Too far to walk, so He send someone."

When they got to Vryheid, they found a man heading to Swaziland, driving a wagonload of corn. He agreed to let them ride along in the wagon. As they rode, Malla pointed out trees and flowers and familiar places, telling interesting stories of her experiences. She was eager to get to Bethel in time for the happy Christmas celebration.

She pointed to the black clouds overhead that threatened rain and said, "Those you will see often. Storms come fast and go fast."

As they stopped for the night, the clouds broke in a furious storm, sending them running for shelter. Malla shouted above the pounding rain. "You will get used to this. Sudden storms go as soon as they come with no damage."

Her words were cut off by Mina's scream. "Malla!"

Malla whirled to see Gina lying on the ground, killed instantly by a bolt of lightning. As the two women stood in the pouring rain with thunder and lightning breaking about them, the wagon driver grabbed them and pulled them under the shelter of the wagon.

"If you stay by those trees you also will be killed," he exclaimed, his face white at the thought of their narrow escape.

They all sat under the wagon, not talking, shaken by what had happened. When the storm rumbled away, the wagon driver took a shovel and walked over to a spot under the branches of a big tree.

"He can't—we're not going to—how can we leave Gina here?" Mina cried.

"She is not here," Malla answered gently.

"I know. But—" Mina covered her face with her hands.

"We can do nothing else," Malla explained. "We cannot take body with us. There no way to send body back." She put a comforting arm around Mina. "This happen many times. We say yes to God, but we not know what He plan for us. We only say to God, Have your way. That best."

The rest of the trip to the border of Swaziland seemed longer than Malla remembered it. There the wagon driver unloaded his corn and turned around to go back. Before starting the oxen, he watched the two women and those carrying their belongings as they started on the two-day walk to Bethel. He shook his head, admiring them but not understanding them.

Malla and Mina arrived in Bethel two days after Christmas. For Malla, the joy of returning to beloved friends eased the tragic loss of Gina. She was home again. But Mina was numbed by suddenly losing the one with whom she had expected to share the newness of missionary life. Gradually she found comfort in the warm welcome of the Christians, both black and white.

"I can see why you were so eager to come back," she said to Malla one day several weeks later.

"But it not the same," Malla burst out. "It different!"

"How?"

Malla gestured around. "New buildings. New people. Praise God for new converts, but—but— some not know me. I not know them. I used to know everyone. Everyone need me."

Johane heard her and exclaimed, "But now there are more missionaries to help. Mr. Dawson did a wonderful work, Teacher. In the first months after you were gone, he baptized sixty converts. And the outstation work—you must see it. It has grown so much. Mr. Dawson deserves to get away on a rest now you are back. You can carry on his work."

Malla turned abruptly and strode away, her shoulders stiff. Johane ran after her. "What is it? You are angry with me."

"Not with you, no." Her voice was cold.

"What then?"

She turned to face him. "This not Mr. Dawson's work. This *my* work. *I* start it. I work alone all those years. Now you—even you—say it his work." She stopped, her voice shaking. "It no longer like old days here. Everyone else make decisions. No one ask me about things. There is no more spirit of love and harmony when I make decision and you do them, Johane."

"But the work has grown so much," he protested. "It is not the same."

"Maybe it should not grow so much," she snapped back.

"And now we have money that you have raised in America," Johane hurried on. "You do not know how hard it was here the years you were gone. We had no rain those years. The grasshoppers took what little was in the fields. People had nothing to wear. We could not even give new converts pieces of cloth to cover them. But you—you bring money, much money."

"When we poor, then we look to the Lord," she insisted, the familiar stubbornness in her voice. "Now people jealous if one neighbor has more than another."

The money Malla had raised during her furlough in America continued to cause problems. Some of the churches in America that sent funds demanded a strict accounting. They were afraid that Malla was not spending the money the way they wanted her to. She had to constantly send assurances in her letters.

"I must help many with money for food, so don't get worried that I am getting too much money. I do not use it for myself, but for the Lord to help the poor people out here."

Even more of a problem was the unrest among other missionaries. One of them was appointed to talk with her and came hesitantly, yet with indignation.

"We feel the funds you receive are sent for the general work here, not just to be used for your station at Bethel."

"The money comes because I spend many months traveling and speaking. I make known the work—*my* work," she interrupted.

"That is where the trouble lies. It is not your work; it is God's work."

"The people in churches in America give money to me. They say I must use it as I want," she answered stubbornly. "If I share with all of you, it not be right to those who send. You have people who send to you."

The missionary tried to keep her voice calm as she said, "Most of us do not have as many people supporting us as you do. We understand that people know about your work and love you, and so they give. We are glad for that. We must feel that you have more than enough funds for the work here. The rest of us have to divide money among many stations."

Malla shook her head, her lips set in a straight line. "The money sent to me. I do not spend on myself. It is for the work. This work." And she gestured at the activity going on around them.

The criticism of her fellow missionaries hurt more than she was willing to admit. "At least there is Johane," she reminded herself. "He still comes for counsel."

As though in answer to that comforting thought, Johane said one evening, "Teacher, I—" he stopped, his voice sounding shy and uncertain "—I do not know if you will like this, but I—I am thinking of getting married."

"Johane! That splendid idea! It mean much to the work if you have wife and family."

"That is what I thought." He grinned back, pleased at her enthusiastic agreement.

"Now I look for wife for you."

"Oh, but, Miss Moe—"

"Leave plans to me, Johane. Think how I help you all these years. Would I stop now? I help you on so important a step."

Johane's shoulders slumped, and he turned and walked slowly away. Watching him, Malla nodded. "He does need wife. I find right one for him."

Her quick mind flew over the names of women who would make him a good wife and immediately found the answer. She ran after him. "Johane, it best you marry the daugther of Zulu chief. I know the right one."

He turned to her, his mouth set in a determined line, but with a mixture of anger and hurt showing in his eyes. "I do not want to marry that one. The Lord has been showing me another girl."

"Who?"

"Sarah Shongwe. I have watched her, and I see how she would make a good wife for me."

"No, Johane. She would not be right for you." She patted his arm. "Do not worry. I make a trip to Natal and find you wife."

Several weeks later Johane received a letter containing pictures of two girls. Malla's words were peremptory. "Hurry, Johane. Decide which girl you like and send word. I am here only a few weeks more. I bring the girl with me to save you trip for her."

Johane sent word that he did not want either girl as a wife. Malla returned to Bethel, expressing her disappointment not only to Johane but to anyone who would listen. Finally, a missionary who had just come to work at Bethel spoke up. "Miss Moe, you are trying to marry Johane to a girl of your choice instead of the one he believes God is giving him."

"I know what is best for Johane—"

"Do you know better than God?" Even though the question was asked gently, it was probing.

Malla turned away without answering. So Johane was going to have his own way and not take her advice. Then he would have to bear the results of his mistake. She would say no more.

The way to cure her disappointment over Johane was to keep busy. And she found much to do. She was well into the work again after furlough. Now she had a grasp of the language, and she understood African customs.

This made it possible for her to accept the many invitations that poured in from kraals in the surrounding countryside. If a horse or mule was available, she rode it to distant places. More often she simply called her helpers together and started out along the uneven roads or across the trackless rocky hills. If no one was free to go with her, she went alone—a small, determined figure in a worn dress and plain coat, often black since it would not show the dirt easily. An umbrella helped to ward off both the blazing sun and the heavy rains. When necessary, she used it as a cane to help her over the rough roads. She always carried a supply of vaseline to rub on her aching feet at night.

Her feet might ache at night, but she could walk fast all day long and not seem tired. One young Swazi convert came running to Johane one day, his Bible open to Romans 10:15. He spelled out the words carefully. "'How beautiful are the feet of them that preach the gospel of peace, and bring glad tidings of good things.' This written about Miss Teacher Moe," he said, nodding confidently.

Malla preached anywhere. It didn't matter to her if she was in a smoke-dim grass hut or out in the open with the noise of crying babies, chirping birds, and restless cattle.

And she always got an audience. Sometimes she stopped in a kraal where she was known, and people flocked to hear her out of love. Often she came to a kraal where she had not been before, and people came out of curiosity. As soon as someone spotted a lone white woman on foot wearing many long heavy dark clothes in the heat of the day, a shout of laughter brought the rest of the village to see her.

Then they found that she ate their food without spitting out the sour milk, she sat with them on their bug-infested mats, and slept on the floor in their huts. No one could keep from asking questions to find out what brought her to them. They listened as she preached the gospel message simply, with the many allegories that helped them understand the message about God's love.

Johane had taught her how to get the message across before the one she was talking to changed the subject. She knew that the queen of a kraal claimed to be the one who sent rain, so she would ask, "Who sends the rain?" When the queen replied that she did, Malla would ask, "Then who makes it rain in other places?" The logical step then was to speak of the great God who made all things.

She used visuals the people could understand. When a rainstorm threatened, she cupped her ear at the sound of thunder and said, "Now—listen. You hear God's great power?"

Her letters home said over and over again, "People in darkness here. They need to know how to get saved. It make no difference how simple the message if God is in it."

Even when she was tired after miles of walking, she would urge herself and her helpers on. "Traveling and preaching in Africa hard on body but good for soul. We go one more kraal. This my opportunity. Perhaps I never see those people again. Perhaps no one else come to them."

When she went back to Bethel after several months' absence, it was only to gather supplies for another trip. And each time she returned to the station, she found Johane and Sarah there to welcome her. And one day Malla threw her arms around Sarah. "Forgive me. I so sorry I didn't want you for Johane. But now I see that you a true Christian. We become good friends."

The missionaries in South Africa were stunned when war broke out in Europe. When it threatened to engulf all of Africa in 1915, Malla agreed with mission headquarters that the feet that had taken her so many miles needed rest. She made the rounds of the stations once more, telling her helpers, "You are my feet to preach to these people while I away."

In June 1915, she boarded the ship that would once again take her to America. She was going on furlough, but not to rest. She never rested from her main job of winning people to Christ. As she walked the decks on the slow journey home, she found that the ship's crew was made up mostly of sailors from India, who knew very little English. Even though she knew no words to speak directly to them about Christ, she showed her friendliness. And she developed a friendship with the tall English captain.

She discovered that the ship was to stop first in Boston, where she was to get off, and then it would continue to New York. She made a note of when the ship would reach New York and where it would dock.

One of her first speaking engagements was at an Evangelical Free Church in New Jersey. She called the pastor of the church early Monday morning and asked him to meet her and another pastor in New York, not telling him the reason. The two men accompanied Malla with her outdated clothes and big black handbag on the train ride to New York. They still didn't know what she wanted them to do.

In New York, they followed her in the sweltering August sun as she darted in and out of bookstores. Finally, at the American Bible Society, she bought one hundred New Testaments in a particular Indian dialect. She asked the clerk to wrap the Bibles in packages of twenty-five each. The two pastors carried the packages as they followed her rapid pace to the subway. They came up in a warehouse district and walked many blocks to a long pier, where the ship from Durban was docked.

When they came in sight of the ship, the crew swarmed around Malla. She tore the wrappings off the New Testaments, and the two pastors handed the Bibles to the sailors. They watched in amazement as the sailors kissed the books and then patted Malla's cheeks in gratitude.

The captain watched, smiling, and said to the pastors, "She is one of the most unique persons I have ever met."

The two men looked at one another. "I think this shows how fast she intends to move during the four years of furlough."

He didn't know how prophetic his words were. Most of Malla's time was spent in the Chicago area, because she wanted to see as much of her family as possible. Her welcome home from Karin was warm. But Dorothea made clear that she still resented what she thought was Malla's desertion of her. She had other feelings about Malla also. She was now a successful teacher, and she was embarrassed not only by Malla's old-fashioned clothes but also by her constant talking about God to everyone she met. Malla didn't hesitate to hand out tracts, whether to a policeman directing traffic on a busy Chicago street or to a woman in a mink coat shopping in a department store.

"Malla, please! Don't be so conspicuous," Dorothea pleaded.

"Most important business is to talk about Jesus," Malla answered.

Late in 1920 Malla realized that her health was breaking under the constant traveling and speaking across America. She made plans to go once more to Norway. She wanted to see friends and familiar places and let the people in cold churches there have a glimpse of the fire God had lighted in Africa. She was only fifty-seven. "I have many years left for God."

9

Malla got home to Norway in time for a happy Christmas family reunion. She had looked forward to spending time on the big Moe farm and seeing new nephews and nieces. But she had also dreaded the year she would be there, because she remembered the coldness and ritual of the State church. She went with her family to the service on Easter Sunday and said, "It is as I feared. Nothing about power of God to change people."

Then, unexpectedly, she heard that special revival meetings were to be held in the school basement. "God, is this a place you use me?" With that prayer in her heart she went to the evangelist to ask if there was some way she could help in the meetings.

He grabbed her hand in both of his and shook it warmly. "I know you," he exclaimed. "I have just read an article about you, telling of your work in Africa. Of course we can use you."

"But people here say methods I use there not work here."

The evangelist shook his head. "We want people to be saved. That was your purpose in Africa. Pastor Ludwig Johnson, who wrote the article, said that you did not go out to scatter the sheep but to gather them in. That is what we are doing in these meetings. We can use you."

"Good. I visit. I know how to do that. I invite people come to meetings."

Malla followed the methods she had used all those long years in Africa. She walked where she could, urging people to pray and read their Bible and attend the meetings. And she hired a farmer to drive her to homes that were too far away for her to walk.

She was so happy she found herself bouncing into each new day, eager to see whom God was going to save that day. Tears of joy ran down her face as she saw people in her beloved country turning from a cold, formal worship to accept the joy and assurance of salvation.

"That happen to me, too, thirty-five, forty years ago. All grace of God."

In the middle of all her busyness, she fell and broke her hip and was forced to stay in bed. Recovery was so slow that she began to think she would never walk again. One sister was worried about her going back to her strenuous life in Africa and suggested that she stay in Norway. "Wouldn't you like to stay here with us until you die?"

Malla's reply was indignant. "I come home for visit, not to die!"

But her long days of slow recovery gave her time to think back over her life. She realized that she had given herself so completely to Africans that she had forgotten her own people and their desperate need for Christ. She began to witness more freely than ever, urging everyone she met, whether friend or casual acquaintance, to "get saved."

In spite of the excitement of the revival in Norway, Malla was impatient to return to Africa. She took a boat from London in October 1922, not knowing that many people did not want her back on the field. The Africans had let her boss them through the years even when they did not understand the reasons for what she did. They simply shrugged their shoulders at requests they considered unreasonable and did what she said. They knew they owed their changed lives to the sacrifices she had made for them.

Her fellow missionaries were not so easily managed. No one who accepted the challenge and went out to the hard life in Swaziland was a follower of anyone except the Lord. Each had gifts and abilities of his own that were independent of Malla. They did not take kindly to her constant efforts to bend everyone to what she thought was God's will for them.

"We don't want her back," they said bluntly to mission headquarters when they heard she planned to return. "She has been on furlough now for six years. The work has grown and is in hands as capable as hers. If she comes back, she will just stir up a lot of problems."

"What exactly do you object to?" The mission leaders wrote back. "Think of her zeal. Her desire to do God's work is the heart of all she does. If you could see how people respond to her over here when she talks about the work. One of her greatest accomplishments is getting people to volunteer to be missionaries."

"But she has no tact! No consideration for others. She's so impatient, so critical, so sharp-tongued. She may love the Africans, but she certainly does not show love to her fellow missionaries."

Some of the missionaries disagreed, saying, "That really is too severe. We can see that some of her attitudes are the result of the years she was here alone. We understand and appreciate that she thinks of this work as hers—"

"Which it isn't," someone else broke in.

"In the twenty years since she came here, many changes have taken place. She sees the changes and the way the work has grown, but she thinks she can still run it alone by giving orders to everyone."

Mr. Dawson's voice was troubled as he said, "My wife and I have known Malla for a long time. She is bossy and tactless and quick to criticize. But so many times I have seen her genuine love for the people. Her whole purpose in life is to see them come to Christ. Can't we be charitable toward her for that reason?"

His words sobered the others, and they nodded slowly. He went on, "I don't think Malla is the only problem we face, or even the main problem. The whole work here in Swaziland is growing so rapidly that it is changing in ways we haven't experienced up to now. I believe we must let the mission board know some of the growing problems we're facing. They may require a change in policy. We need someone to come from the home office to give us direction."

In response to a letter from the missionaries, Pastor Ludwig Johnson came out to Swaziland in 1921. He urged more acceptance of Malla, reminding them of her love for people. Most of all his messages from God's Word gave a sense of unity and harmony to the missionary group. Under his leadership they made plans to begin a new Bible school.

Opposition to Malla's return evaporated in their renewed dedication to God. As she walked the deck of the ship, eager to reach her beloved Bethel, she was unaware of how nearly her missionary career had ended.

The two men who were to head up the new school, Arthur Jensen and M.D. Christensen, were young men experienced in both business and Christian work. Both knew how to use the abilities of their fellow workers. Mr. Christensen had heard Malla speak and had volunteered for mission work in Swaziland in response to her message.

When he and Mr. Jensen met Malla on her return, they soon understood why she had irritated others who had to work closely with her. Her domineering, tactless exterior was prickly. But they saw beyond it to the great desire she had to win people to Christ. It did not excuse the impatience she showed to others, but it made understandable the times she rode rough-shod over another person's opinion.

Mr. Jensen often stopped at the Bethel station to help Malla do jobs that needed a man's strength. He was able to persuade her to stay in her own territory and not try to run the work of other stations. His methods worked because Malla respected him, not realizing that he was always alert to smooth relations between her and other missionaries.

So the first months of the third term of the sixty-year-old missionary saw her mellowing a litte. Mr. Jensen went out of his way to praise her to other missionaries, helping those who didn't know her well to see her good qualities. And, while Malla could not rid herself of the lifelong urge to manage everyone and everything around her, her manner softened so that other missionaries found her interference less irritating.

Emma Dawson said impulsively one day, "I'm glad the home board decided to let you come back, Malla."

"Of course I come back." Malla turned, a questioning frown on her face. "Let me come back? What you mean? Did they think because I sick in Norway I not want to come back to hard work?"

"Uh—no. I—I mean—"

But Malla's direct gaze didn't waver as she demanded, "Emma, we work together from beginning. Tell me. Was there idea I not be allowed to return? Tell me why."

Emma's stammered explanation as she tried to be kind was clear to Malla. Her fellow missionaries hadn't wanted her. She was hurt and angry and defensive and felt her old burden of depression sweep over her. She wanted to run and hide where no one could see her tears.

Instead, she went to Mr. Jensen and asked bluntly, "Is it true I almost kept home by mission board because no one here want me?"

He was equally honest, telling her of the resentment some of the other workers felt toward her. "But you are not like that so much now, Malla."

"That because of you, dear friend," she replied. "You open to me a new way of love and understanding when we work with people. How I miss you when you go on furlough."

"I may be gone, but God is here as always." Then he smiled at her. "I've got a surprise for you."

"I not like surprises," she answered, her voice showing her suspicion.

"Unless they are your idea?" Mr. Jensen teased. "You will like this one. I have got you a one-horse carriage big enough to carry you and a helper or two and your baggage on your treks to distant kraals. We do not want you walking so much."

Malla felt a moment of indignation that he thought her age was slowing her down. Then a new thought came, and she exclaimed, "That mean I visit more places. I go then so much farther than I go on foot. Thanks be to God."

Malla found her outreach constantly widening.

When she went to the many stations that were established far from Bethel, she found that she knew the pastors of the churches. Many of them were young men who had been saved at Bethel years before. Often they had carried her bundles as she walked from one kraal to another. They had listened as she won people to Christ, and now they were following her steps.

Often they said, "We remember how you prayed. We heard you say, 'My soul hungry to help lost sinners. My soul is crying. I feel bad because people not want to be saved. When we see people saved, we forget all hardship.' Often you did not eat or sleep, but prayed. We never forget your example."

One day a new missionary came to Swaziland and stayed in a home where Malla was also a guest. Everything was new and different to the visitor, and she found the countryside more beautiful than she had expected. She looked out the window one morning and exclaimed, "Aren't those hills beautiful? I don't think I'll ever get tired of looking at them."

Malla walked over to stand beside her. "Yah. They are beautiful to look at. But there much in them that not so nice to see. Much darkness there. I see lost souls in beautiful hills. That God save them all is my cry."

Then before the missionary could reply, Malla leaned forward to peer out the window. "Someone there. Quick! Make tea. I run out to invite person in."

"Who is it? Someone you know?"

Malla shook her head impatiently. "No, but maybe it someone who not know Christ. We give tea so that he must sit still to hear how to be saved. Quick now!"

When the new missionary first came to the Bethel

station, Malla was away, and she had heard stories about her that she thought couldn't possibly be true. As she sat in her room one day struggling with language study, she could hear Malla talking outside the front door. Two little boys had come asking for a match box. She heard Malla answer, "If you kneel down and pray and give heart to Jesus, I give you match box."

The missionary hurried to the window and watched the two boys kneel. They repeated the words Malla told them and then ran off, each with a match box. She shook her head in protest. How could Malla do that? After all her years on the mission field, she should know that you couldn't bribe people to believe. Other missionaries had told her of this habit Malla had, and now she had seen it for herself.

She turned around when Malla hurried into the room and said triumphantly, "Two more souls for Jesus."

"But—how do you know they really believed? All they wanted was to get you to give them a match box."

"Oh, I watch them now. I will see. Then I speak to them again. I say to them, remember you ask Jesus in your heart. You must live different. But for today—" she shrugged "—prayer always come more easily after they get some little thing." Then, seeing the doubt on the missionary's face, she added, "No one really saved, I think, unless they show signs. There must be love to others. They must turn from sin, make good earlier mistakes."

The missionary went back to her language study, admiring Malla's zeal even though she still thought her method was wrong. She giggled suddenly as she remembered what she had seen the day before.

Malla had met a man on the street and had taken

his hand when he reached to shake hers. Then, before he realized what was happening, she had dropped to her knees. Because she was holding his hand in a firm girp, he was pulled to the ground also and had to listen while she prayed for him. Coming into the house later, Malla had said with great satisfaction, "He will not forget prayer. Now he think about God."

"I don't think I'll ever be able to talk to people as freely as you do," the missionary had answered.

Then Malla had sat down across the table from her. "Soulwinning not hard if God push you. When I see how little effort it take to win souls, I tremble. I think of many opportunities I miss. We must do the little things. We only tell about God. We cannot save. I go to visit in jail. Guard say no prisoners there then. I say to him, 'If you not saved, you are prisoner.' Later he come to meeting and is saved."

She got up to walk around the room, her actions restless. "I have been here long time. I know how powerful is pull of old life. Heathen culture strong. New convert must say so right away so people know and watch. When signs of old life come back, we see and talk. I not count someone for sure until I see him safely over. That the reason I like funerals of believers. Whenever I go to funeral of believer I say, "Now he safe. Praise God."

10

Just before noon one day in 1927, Malla walked into a neighboring station in time for lunch.

"Malla! How did you get here? Surely you didn't walk the twelve miles from Bethel in the hot sun? I hope at sixty-five you know better," her missionary friend scolded gently.

"No, I have run part of the way," Malla answered. "I meet people on the way who get saved. Praise God. But I come to tell you idea I have. I have way to reach more people. Now that I sixty-five, I must use head." Her eyes twinkled as she answered.

"Will your idea keep until after lunch? We are just ready to sit down."

"I talk while we eat after we pray." She began immediately, as she helped herself to food. "I plan to build Gospel Wagon."

"What do you mean?"

"A week ago I sit and think back. Long time ago Lizzie and Emelia and some others go out in wagon. They carry supplies and stay few months at once. So I think, I do that too. I will build house, a small house on wheels so I go faster than by foot. I can live in it. I will be like turtle, carrying house with me. If big enough, I carry supplies for three or four month trek so I not come back to Bethel so many times. And I use it when someone need private conversation, more private than out under trees."

Someone at the table said cautiously, "But won't a wagon like that cost a lot of money to build?"

"A mission group in America send money for what I need now that I older. I think of Gospel Wagon."

"It would be hard to get something very big through the thick underbrush and under tree branches. And if it is very wide, it will get stuck along the narrow paths."

"And what about fording the rivers? You will need big wheels to set the wagon high enough to keep it out of the water."

"I know. I know." Malla's answer was impatient. She knew everyone was shaking his head doubtfully over the crazy idea. But she held to it stubbornly. She found a teacher at the Franson Memorial Bible School and convinced him of her vision. He drew the plans, under her directions, and persuaded a firm in Durban to build it. Then came the day when it stood tall and impressive in the yard at Bethel.

"Just look at those wheels!" Johane exclaimed. "They will easily roll over the tall grass and go safely through the rivers. How tall is the wagon?"

"From the ground to the top it eight feet. And from the front to the door in back it ten feet. See how grand?" Malla answered proudly.

"How do you get into it?" one of the helpers asked. "That's too big a step for you from the ground. Someone will have to boost you in."

"No, no. There are steps hidden here." Malla excitedly showed the four steps at the rear door, which folded up under the wagon. "And see—two closets to store clothes and extra supplies. And more cabinets here. And my bed turns into a seat in daytime. Here shelves for books, and here a table when I not want to eat outside."

"Malla, you have not said who will go along to help. You will need a driver, and someone to care for the donkeys, and—"

"I have all ready now," she said triumphantly. "Sonias is to drive, and you know he is good. Mafika will lead donkeys. I have Josephine to cook. Lizzie and Leah from nearby kraal come to be general help."

It took a year for Malla to get everything ready. Whenever she put anything into the Gospel Wagon, everyone who had a minute to spare came to watch. She put in her big iron pot for cooking and numerous smaller pans and water containers. She kept a long list and checked off supplies. A big bag of corn meal was needed as the staple for meals. Her helpers loaded in 200 pounds of salt and a big supply of matches, these for bait to lure people to listen to the messages.

Someone looked into the wagon and asked, "What are all those old clothes for?"

"I hand out to people God going to give me to be saved."

"How will you get more supplies if you run out?" someone else asked. "You have a lot there, but it won't last as long as you plan to be gone."

"We find store to get more beans. Or we stop at kraal and barter salt for meat and eggs. Sometimes chiefs give gifts, especially chicken. And I bake good bread in my big iron pot."

Finally the day came when the Gospel Wagon was ready for the adventure. Everyone on the station crowded around for prayer. The eight pairs of donkeys stood patiently in harness, the driver took the reins, and the wagon slowly rolled down the path. The donkeys plodded along, with Malla leading everyone in singing what she called the official traveling hymn.

> "Go with me, go with me.
> Savior, walk with me.
> I have no strength to walk alone.
> Savior, walk with me."

Everyone standing in the yard at Bethel listened until they could hear the singing no longer.

Those who knew Malla well would have been surprised if they had heard the words she spoke half aloud as the wagon creaked along. "How I know this work?" she asked herself. "Gospel Wagon all paid for. I have plenty helpers. All so glad to come along. You know, God, I can no longer walk so far. My body old, but my spirit young. Now, God, You send people You want to be saved."

Malla soon discovered that the main drawback to the Gospel Wagon was its slow progress. The donkeys' short legs made them take short steps. Sometimes the rocking motion of the wagon bothered Malla. Every now and then she got out and walked ahead to rest under a tree until the wagon caught up with her.

Sonias found it was not easy to push a wide wagon through the brush and over roads that were only narrow paths made for feet, not wagon wheels. He frequently had to get down from the driver's seat and cut down trees in order to move along the path.

Malla had planned the procedure they would follow on the trip just as carefully as she had chosen supplies and helpers. Each member of the group had definite responsibilities. They planned to stop each day within easy walking distance of a kraal—a large one, if possible. The Gospel Wagon then would be the central spot from which the helpers could fan out to other nearby kraals.

"Now we get busy," Malla always said when Sonias pulled the donkeys to a stop. She stepped briskly down the back steps of the wagon and looked around. "Yah, this good spot. Plenty trees for shade." She made sure her hat was on and tucked her big purse under her arm, checking to see that it bulged with small gifts for anyone she met on the way.

"First I walk to kraal. Not nice to come riding. Better to come walking." And she started off along the path almost on a run, eager to see what God was going to do at this time in this place. It was always exciting to wonder if this would be the kraal of a chief she didn't know and could introduce to Jesus or the kraal of a chief she had met so she could check his growth in the Lord and give encouragement.

While she was gone, the helpers got busy with their duties. The boys took care of any repairs the wagon might need and looked after the donkeys.

Josephine and the other girls did the cooking for the day. She always brewed a big kettle of tea to have ready for the visitors she knew would swarm around as soon as word got out that something strange stood in the path near the kraal.

But the helpers were not along only to prepare food for the bodies of the people. One person always stayed at the wagon to welcome visitors with tea and bread and an invitation to be saved. The others went out to visit and evangelize. Sometimes Sonias and the others took beds and walked miles to kraals that were far from the road where the Gospel Wagon was parked.

"This not vacation trip," Malla frequently reminded everyone. "We here on business for God."

Malla had planned a definite route through Swaziland, but she did not follow a rigid schedule. There was no set limit to the number of miles they traveled in a day. She had some definite places she wanted to visit, but if people turned up unexpectedly, the wagon stopped for as long as necessary.

"As long as people come to hear of God, we stay and talk," Malla insisted. "We have plenty food, good place to sleep, nice weather. God is with us. What more we need?"

"But you know a lot of these people come just because they smell the bread baking in your big iron pot," one of the helpers protested one day.

"Yah, would you not come for such good smell?" Malla retorted. "The reason make no difference so they come. I bake bread in hot sun all day if it bring someone to hear gospel."

Malla was eager to get to Queen Lomawa's large kraal where she would feel at home. Queen Lomawa had been saved as a young girl on one of Malla's visits and called her "my white mother."

Many hundreds came to hear the preaching. But they were mostly interested in how the wagon worked. They peered in the two small windows, climbed up to rap the top with their knuckles, and peered underneath to see how the four steps folded under the bottom of the wagon. Malla and the helpers were always quick to offer every visitor tea or coffee and bread. African politeness then required that, having eaten her food, they must stay to hear her preach.

Every new believer was given a gift of clothing. Malla thought she had brought a large enough supply to last her for the trip. But as they moved along from one kraal to another, she became worried.

"I not have faith enough," she said. "So many people get saved, I not have clothes enough."

She turned and looked at Josephine. "You and Lizzie and Leah have extra dress?"

"Yes, Miss Moe. So we have a change."

"You give me. I give out to someone."

"But, Miss Moe, we need it."

She brushed aside their protests. "These brand new Christians. You old ones. We give something so they know we love them. You not mind lose clothes for sake of gospel?"

Put on that basis, the girls couldn't argue, especially when they knew Miss Moe gave away her clothes, too.

Malla looked out and said, "Quick, Josephine, I need dress. Here comes woman."

"But there are two women, Miss Moe."

Malla stood looking at the dress in her hand. Then with a sudden motion she tore it in two. "There. Now we have more to give," she said, as she handed the top to one woman and the skirt to the other. She looked in astonishment at Josephine, who stood giggling helplessly.

"What will she do when two men come needing trousers?" Josephine asked Leah when Malla was out of hearing.

Malla did not give away many clothes at Queen Lomawa's kraal. Though many came to look and listen, they were not interested in the preaching. The queen invited Malla to talk with her each day and gave her a generous supply of pumpkins, corn, milk, and meat.

Malla watched as the queen eased herself slowly down to the ground to sit and talk. "Your back hurt bad?" Malla asked.

"I cannot sleep comfortably any longer on the sleeping mat," the queen answered, rubbing her back.

Malla turned to one of her helpers. "Run quick and bring mattress from my bed," she ordered. When the young man returned, Malla went with the queen to her hut and spread the mattress out on the queen's sleeping mat. "Now you will sleep."

"But what will you do?"

She shrugged. "I find another mattress." When she finished talking to the queen, Malla went back to the wagon. She spent the rest of the day sewing empty sacks together and filling them with corn husks for a mattress for herself.

Leaving the queen's kraal one day, Malla saw the chief of a nearby kraal coming out of curiosity to see the much-talked about wagon. Her African helpers watched in shock as she ran to him and grabbed his arm to lead him over to the wagon. She explained how it worked, still holding his arm in a firm grasp. Then she sank to her knees, pulling him down with her, and broke into a loud prayer.

The bewilderment on his face when the prayer was over and Malla pulled him to his feet again was so comical that her helpers had to turn away to hide their smiles, even though they were a little afraid that he might be angry. Something in Malla's smile and enthusiasm reached the chief, and he agreed that she could come to his kraal and preach all she wanted.

But after they had been in the kraal a few days, Malla became restless. The chief's wives were not coming to see the wagon or to hear the messages. She called Johane and Sonias and told them to go to the wives' hut and preach to the women.

"We cannot! We dare not!" they exclaimed in horror. "Miss Moe, you know that no man can enter a hut where the women are. The chief's wives, especially, are protected. We cannot do what you ask."

"The chief has said to preach in his kraal."

"But he did not say to his women," Sonias protested.

"He not tell me *not* to preach to wives. So you go."

Sonias and Johane turned reluctantly and fearfully to walk to the wives' hut. They were so used to doing what Malla told them to do that obeying her was more important than their fear of breaking long-standing customs. And anyway, they had seen so often that God was with Malla. Hadn't she just dragged the chief to his knees to pray for him, and he had not been angry?

When they came back, their faces wore broad grins. "Some of the women believed us. And some children too. They were sorry they had been too lazy to come to the Gospel Wagon, and they said they would come tomorrow. How glad we are that you made us go."

"You see? God stronger than chief. He wanted women to hear and be saved. He protected you. Always trust God."

Finally Malla was ready for the return trip, satisfied with what God had done. The way back was slow, as they stopped frequently. But at last Sonias turned the weary donkeys into the yard at Bethel, and the travelers climbed out to a warm welcome from those whc had traveled with them in their thoughts and prayers.

"You see? Gospel Wagon works. Trip through Swaziland success. Thousands hear about Jesus who otherwise maybe never hear. Praise God."

11

But Malla was not satisfied. She began thinking about Tongaland, a six-hundred-square-mile area east of the tall, forbidding Ubombo Mountains. "Ten thousand people there," she mused. "They not yet know of Christ. Too hard for missionaries to live there. I go in Gospel Wagon."

When she told her plans, she got the exclamations of protest from everyone that she expected.

"You can't go there! The country is full of malaria seven or eight months out of every year. You can't risk getting malaria at your age."

"I already live in Africa thirty-six years and not be sick. Except a little. God look after me then; He take care of me now."

"Malla, there is a shortage of both water and food in that country. Life is too dangerous there for you. Be sensible. Don't try going to Tongaland."

"And the roads, if you can call them that," someone else said. "They are terrible, hardly passable."

"People there also who not hear of Christ," Malla answered simply, with the stubborn note in her voice that meant she was determined to go. She went ahead making plans for the trip in spite of the pleas of her friends.

She marked off on her fingers the answer to each objection. "You say no way to go. I say Gospel

Wagon take me and keep me safe. You say no place to live. I live in wagon. You say not enough food and water. I take plenty supplies along in wagon. God go with us as always. Johane go this time as preacher. Sonias is good driver. He learn much from last trip. Josephine and Leah good cooks. They all experienced now."

"When do you plan to leave?" her friends asked, knowing it wouldn't do any good to argue with her any longer.

"We get ready in June to reach Tongaland for winter months. The low lands hot and dry then, and not so much danger of fever."

"But that is the very worst time of year!" The objections came thick and fast again. "You won't be able to replenish your water supplies because the rivers will be dried up. The only streams available will be the waterholes of the hippos and rhinoceros. The water won't be fit to drink. You'll die of thirst."

"We have face that other times," Malla answered. "Leah and Josephine know to dip out much mud and slime on top of water before filling containers. They know to boil water first and put in lemon juice to make it good to drink. It slow, but it work."

"Tell us at least how long you plan to stay."

"When the dry winter end, we start back to Swaziland. We back track part of way. That way we see again those saved on way out. We see how they do. They need encouragement by then," she finished, nodding wisely.

"So if you are out of Tongaland by the end of August when winter ends, you should be back here in Bethel by the middle of September. Can we count on seeing you then?" her friends persisted.

"Oh, yah, certainly by end of September," Malla agreed. Then she added a word of caution. "I cannot be sure when we reach here. It depend on people we meet on way home. Some may need long time to talk."

When it came time to load the wagon, Malla left nothing to chance. She stood by the door and checked the supplies that were loaded, making sure everything was stored in its proper place. She shook her head at the supply of old clothes. "These people in Tongaland poor. They have nothing. They believe when they hear gospel. We must take many clothes to give."

After she made sure that all the supplies were in place, she checked to see that the donkeys were properly harnessed and that their feet were in good shape for the rough, stony roads they would be walking.

"So, now we go," she finally announced. "We get ready to sing traveling hymn."

The other missionaries and workers stood in the bare yard in front of the Bethel station and watched the wagon turn out of the yard onto the road.

"She is just as stubborn as she gets on toward seventy as she was when she first came to the field at thirty." Emelia sighed.

"Yes, but she is also just as eager to win people to Jesus as she was then," Lizzie reminded her, as she waved until the wagon was lost to sight and the singing could no longer be heard.

Malla had planned a definite first stop. But on the way, a dozen or more stops were made at different kraals. The sound of the creaking wheels carried clearly through the air, and people often dropped what they were doing and came rushing to greet Malla.

Often Malla and her helpers got off the wagon and walked ahead to a kraal. They had time to greet people, leave some gifts, read Scripture and preach a brief message, and then catch up with the wagon a short distance along the road. The first twenty-five miles of this trip to Tongaland wound past the homes of believers who attended services at Bethel. They all wanted a chance to greet Malla, so progress was slow the first few days.

But Malla never minded how slowly they went if it meant she had a chance to talk to people. "This not just a wagon we travel in," she kept reminding her helpers. "This a Gospel Wagon. We travel with good news of Jesus."

By the end of the second day they reached the Pongola River and stopped for the night. They followed the sleeping arrangements that had worked well on the first trip. Malla slept in her bed in the wagon, with Josephine and the three other girls sleeping on mats on the floor. The boys slept on mats under the wagon.

In the morning, as they got ready to cross the river, Malla said, "You see why we come now at beginning of winter months. Is dry now already, and water level low. We cross without trouble."

They made several stops at stations to visit with missionaries, and Malla made use of the kitchens there to bake bread to give to those who came to the wagon.

At last the great mountain range could be seen. Sonias shook his head when he saw the steep, winding, rocky trail the donkeys would have to climb. But Malla encouraged him. "They do God's work, too, Sonias. Do not hit them too hard."

Everyone sighed with relief when they reached the top of the mountain range. They thought the worst was over, until Sonias began to guide the donkeys down the steep rocky slope. Beads of sweat stood out on his face as he worked at the brakes to keep the wagon from rolling downhill too fast.

"Nathaniel, you walk with donkeys so they not get tangled in harness. Sonias good driver. He will keep wagon from rolling off cliff."

Josephine and the other helpers looked at one another. Teacher Moe sounded as though she was sure the wagon wouldn't go over the edge. But they decided to scramble out and walk just in case she was wrong.

"Now we come again to good, flat ground," Malla said when they finally trundled over the level grass-covered land. "Now we find kraals along the way and stop for few weeks."

Finally they moved on again at a slow pace, Malla always alert for the sounds of a village. Sonias shaded his eyes with his hand as he stared out ahead one day. "We're coming to a long stretch of sand. Look, I have never seen sand so white."

"Will it be easy to drive heavy wagon over?"

"I do not know." Sonias flapped the reins over the donkeys' backs and shouted at them to try to speed their pace. But he found the sand so loose and dry that the wheels of the heavy wagon sank deeper and deeper as he drove. Finally everyone, including Malla, got out and walked in order to lighten the load.

Sonias shook his head as he looked at the sand and the distance they still had to travel. "We must build a road to go on. It will take a whole day to chop down trees."

"Good. That give time to see people and talk. That is why we come."

So while Sonias and Nathaniel chopped down trees to make a track for the wagon wheels, Josephine and her helpers brewed tea, and Malla gave out gifts of matches, salt, and sugar to the curious who came to see what was going on. Malla noticed that none of the kraals were near the road, so she ordered, "Watch to see if footpaths lead off wagon trail. Look good, because bushes so thick they hide path."

One morning after they had gone for several hours without seeing anyone, Malla called, "Sonias, stop." She climbed out of the wagon and stood listening, one hand behind her ear. "Listen for sound of rooster. Maybe sound of someone pounding corn in hollow log. Then we know a kraal nearby. Tonga people friendly."

"I only know my Zulu language, and that is Johane's language," Sonias said. "How can we talk to them?"

"We smile and give tea and bread. We not need words for that. Then we point to sky and talk about God. All people want to know about God."

The helpers soon found that Malla was right. When she and Johane preached, the Tongas listened more eagerly than had people in some of the kraals in Swaziland. "How can we be saved?" was the first question they asked. Then the second question came. "If you leave us, who will help us understand more about these things you tell us?"

"Some day someone come live with you," Malla promised. "Someone teach you more." She always was sad at having to make a promise without knowing when it would come true. She could only say, "Do not turn from God. Ask God to teach you."

As the winter season drew to a close, Sonias turned the Gospel Wagon toward Swaziland and home. Malla was glad each time she returned to Bethel. It gave her a chance to see friends and to replenish her supplies for the next trip.

But every time she talked about another trip, someone always protested that she was too old. A letter came from a mission leader saying, "You must rest more. We are praying the Lord will bless you in the evening of your life."

Malla dashed off a quick protest. "Thank you for kind greeting. You know, when it is evening, it soon become dark. I work before it get too dark."

So she went right on with the Gospel Wagon work, sometimes taking shorter trips to visit kraals but spending the winters in Tongaland. Once in a while she went out to visit by bus or asked a missionary to take her in a car. She did that only if she was not feeling strong enough to walk or travel in the wagon.

As she watched missionaries drive from station to station by car, she shook her head disapprovingly. "Motorcar goes too fast by. It not see people. To win souls takes time. We must go slow, have time to talk."

Malla hated to take time for anything that kept her from the important job God had given her. She was invited to special meetings in Johannesburg that would give her a chance to rest and to hear messages from God's Word. But she decided not to go. "It take time to go, and it cost me money. Not good. Both I can use to help someone. God must revive me here."

People had to admit that the ten years of Gospel Wagon ministry had undreamed of results. Africans in Tongaland, Swaziland, and Zululand looked forward to the sound of the lumbering house on wheels, as it jolted its way along the narrow footpaths and splashed its way through the rivers and streams. But most of all, people looked for the little woman in a black dress, who had a big smile as she came down

116

the four steps at the back of the wagon. She gave generous helpings of tea and bread and a simple gift to anyone who came to listen to the gospel story of the Lord Jesus.

"You bring light into our dark huts," one bent old woman told her. "Before, I was afraid to die. Now, I do not want to, but I am not afraid."

"I no longer fear evil spirits," one chief said. "We now have song services instead of beer drinks. We meet for prayer instead of meeting to learn to do black magic." He struggled to find words to express another thought. "Miss Moe said she did not come to change customs of our tribes. She said when we ask Jesus to change our heart, we want to give up the old ways. We know then they are not good."

When Malla and her helpers started on the yearly trip to Tongaland in 1938, they didn't know it would be the last one with the Gospel Wagon. They spent nine weeks in Tongaland in spite of much sickness among the people and among Malla's helpers. Even Malla, who was seldom sick, had boils on different parts of her body. They were so painful that she had to go into the hospital, the first time in her seventy-five years that she had been there as a patient.

Malla was impatient with her slow recovery from the boils and discouraged because she was being kept from the witnessing she so loved to do. When she felt well enough to travel, she went on a brief visit to Durban and met for the first time the carpenters who had built the Gospel Wagon. She wanted to make sure they had the gospel presented to them clearly.

"When I pray with people in Gospel Wagon, I think of you who make such nice wagon for me. Remember Noah's carpenters? They help build ark, but they not get in. You build Gospel Wagon that bring salvation to many. It would be great shame if you not get to heaven because you not believe on Lord Jesus."

She remembered to pray for the brothers when she went home, knowing God could work when she could not.

Now that she did not make as many extended trips with the Gospel Wagon, she was free to visit other stations and give help and advice to newer missionaries—and older ones as well. She couldn't resist giving orders when she saw something that she thought needed doing.

One missionary wife sighed when she saw Malla coming. "I do love her, but she is hard to have as a guest. She just takes over the whole house as though it were hers. But this time she simply must stay out of the kitchen. I have just gotten the cook trained to do things my way."

The wish seemed to work for several days, until the missionary found Malla bustling about in the kitchen, pots and pans everywhere, and the African cook running to get what she needed.

The missionary tried to be tactful as she saw the mess in the kitchen. "Miss Moe, you mustn't tire yourself out."

"Not tired," Malla answered as she stirred a huge bowl of dough. "I just make batch of doughnuts."

"But—so many? We don't have many visitors just now."

"Oh, I make month's supply," Malla answered, pushing back the hair that had slipped from the knot at the back of her head. "No use to make just a few."

The missionary walked away, trying not to explode. "Where can I store a month's supply of doughnuts so they will stay fresh?" she demanded.

Her husband laughed. Then, seeing his wife's indignant face, he said hastily, "I'm not laughing at you. I just heard a story about Miss Moe."

"Let me hear it. I need something to make me laugh at this point."

"I don't know just when this happened. But Mr. Jensen came to Bethel late one night after visiting some of the outstations. He got caught in a violent rainstorm, and his clothes were soaked. Miss Moe insisted he go to bed, and she hung his clothes to dry. When he asked for his clothes the next morning, she said, 'Today you not run off in hurry like you always do. You so busy you not have time to sit and visit with me. This time I keep your trousers, and you stay in bed. That way we have good long talk.'"

His wife laughed. "You even sounded like Miss Moe. Only she would have nerve enough to do that."

"I don't mind admitting that I'm a little worried about what she will take it into her head to do during the dedication of the new government dispensary at the Franson Memorial Bible School. There will be a lot of officials there and many others who aren't familiar with Miss Moe's ways—and people who don't love her as we do."

Other missionaries remembered Malla's impatience with longwinded speakers. They had been present at meetings when she had stood up in the middle of a long sermon and asked the speaker to sit down so someone else could have a chance to speak.

During the conference they put Malla in the middle of a group of missionaries and officials where she could not easily get out. As speaker after speaker was introduced, Malla became increasingly restless. Finally she stood up quickly and clambered over the people near her. She took the master of ceremonies by the arm as he started to introduce the next speaker.

"I say a few words," she said abruptly.

He looked down into her wrinkled face and saw the determination. "Of course," he answered and motioned for the interpreter to stand beside her.

She began in her brand of English, politely recognizing the government officials and speaking mainly to the white people in the audience. The young interpreter hurried to keep up with her rapid speech as he translated into Zulu.

Then, turning to the African audience, she launched into Zulu with the interpreter switching to English. Realizing what she was doing, Malla began speaking English again. The interpreter couldn't keep up with the mixture of English and Zulu and just shrugged his shoulders and sat down. The laughing audience forgot its boredom and listened to Malla's impassioned mixture of languages as she told what God had done among the Swazi and Zulu people and gave a clear gospel message.

"That's exactly what she had in mind all along," one missionary whispered to another, half in exasperation and half in admiration.

As soon as the ceremonies were over, Malla grasped the arm of the chief medical director of Swaziland. "May I talk few minutes about God?" she asked politely. Then, not giving him a chance to answer, she urged him to take Christ as his personal Savior. The man listened and thanked her for her interest.

A young missionary overheard the conversation and later said impulsively, "Oh, Miss Moe, I wish I had your courage to talk to a person like that."

"Courage?" Malla repeated. "I not have courage. I shake the whole time. I afraid of him, but I more afraid of God. God says tell people they must be saved. I obey Him."

12

When Malla was eighty and not going out to visit kraals as often, she had time to think back over her fifty years in Africa.

Some of her memories made her laugh. She listened one day to a new missionary struggling to learn Zulu. She nodded her head in sympathy when the missionary burst out, "I'll never get the clicking sounds right. Like this one I'm supposed to make in the verse, 'Behold, I stand at the door and knock.' I can't get the knocking sound right."

"At least now people know what knock on door means. When Emma went to kraal with me, huts not have doors. We make clicking sounds and people laugh." She stopped to laugh herself. "I still not speak English good after all these years, but I speak good Zulu."

Other memories reminded her of lost opportunities. "I must go see place I visit long ago. Maja, the great chief, was good friend to me. He promised place to build church and school. Mr. Dawson and Emma and Johane go with me. We all go so happy. Then came time for Swazi war, and we not allowed to build."

She shook her head at the sad memory. "I pray for that place on top of mountain fifty years. I like to visit again. Last time I go there, I told people I come back. Maybe God take me home soon, so I not have much time."

"But, Malla, that would be too hard a trip for you."

"If you take me to foot of mountain, I walk rest of way. Dorika and Shabangu help me."

Malla took for granted everyone would agree with her plans, and she set a day for the trip. There was no way to get up the mountain except by foot, and Malla found the climb harder than she remembered.

"I young then," she explained to Dorika and Shabangu, who only smiled at each other over Malla's head. After several long stops to rest, they worked out a system to make faster progress. They went single file with Malla's hands holding Dorika's shoulders and Shabangu coming last to push Malla from behind.

She had a wonderful time in the kraal and couldn't stop talking about it when she got home. "I stayed in nice hut, slept in African bed, ate African food. I thank God even though I old, God use me to help people get saved. All grace of God."

"Did some become saved?"

"Yah, seven people ask to be saved." She shook her head. "I don't know if they stand true, but they willing to make start. We not know if they truly saved. Only God knows that. But we pray God they be kept safe."

After giving this good news about her trip, she asked what had gone on at Bethel in the few weeks she had been gone. Suddenly she exclaimed, "Oh, I forget. A man came to be saved, but said not that day. I there three weeks, and he not come back. He said he come, but I not wait. Oh! Oh!"

She began to cry, "God, You not willing that any perish, not even one. Oh, save him, too, Lord."

122

Her friends tried to comfort her. "Just remember that because you made that hard trip up the mountain, seven people will be in heaven who would not be there if you hadn't gone looking for them."

"But one still out on mountain," she said, tears streaming down her cheeks. "Like lost sheep in Jesus' parable. I must go again to find him."

Finally the others at the station sent a runner to an evangelist, asking him to find the man and pray with him. "I not rest easy in heart until God find him." Her friends knew she would continue to pray for the man until she heard of his salvation.

That unknown man was just as important to her as Dorothea was. All through the long years, wherever she was or however busy, the promise to care for her sister rang in her ears. That promise included more than just the physical care her mother had asked for. To Malla it meant spiritual care. When she received a cable that her sister had died, she burst into tears. Then she saw the news that Dorothea had accepted Christ, and she blurted, "Good news! Dora died saved." She wouldn't let any of her African friends cry with her. "This is time to sing. I pray for fifty years, and now God answered."

She immediately included the news in one of the "circulary" letters that went out to her many friends. Malla had always written letters to thank people for gifts, to give sympathy, to warn about the need to be saved, to report on the work God was doing in Africa. Because she loved to write, she was sure everyone was equally eager to get the letters. She wrote even when she visited distant kraals and was not always able to mail the letters immediately. When this happened she often apologized, "I felt sorry for you not getting letter from me in so long time."

Malla never hesitated to tell people in her home churches in America and Norway about the needs of the work. She just expected that they would want to know the needs. And she took for granted that they would want to help by sending money. After all, she was asking for the Lord's work, not for herself. She wrote, "Without your gifts of money and parcels of clothes you send, I could not give to people who have nothing. Remember, God loves cheerful giver. You want to be loved? Then you give."

Bethel had been Malla's center of activity for so many years that she still felt responsible for everything that went on there, even though others were now in charge. She especially cared deeply for the school. She liked to tell anyone who would listen how she and Johane had started it those many years back.

"We have only two small rooms, one for Johane and boys and one for girls and me. In them we study, we eat, we sleep. So hot it was when sun beat down on roof. Only few students came because fathers not want children in school. Parents afraid they become Christians. So they come often to take children out. Then Johane go with me to ask can they come back. We must take all care for them — grow food, make clothes."

Malla looked around, her eyes squinting in the sun. She gestured at the school building. "All so different now."

Then she heard the school bell ring and frowned as she saw the boys and girls pour out of the building, shouting as they ran to the field to play games. She shook her head and tightened her lips in disapproval. "Play all work of Satan. Games and sports is waste of time. Knitting for girls and carpentry for boys waste of time. Education important, not play.

Students must know God's Word and how to tell people way to God."

There was one story other missionaries liked to tell gleefully, but never in Malla's hearing. She had finally told everyone that she was reconciled to the fact that time was set aside in the school day for play, even though she didn't approve of it.

"Then one day she caught some boys playing football on Sunday. She marched out to the field, grabbed the ball, and took it into the house. None of the boys dared stop her. For one thing, they respected her, and then too—well, they were probably a little bit scared of her."

"Did she ever give them back the football?"

"It wouldn't have done them any good if she had, because she took a big kitchen knife and cut it into tiny pieces." The one telling the story chuckled as he added, "She no doubt gave the boys something else to make up for it."

Someone else took up the story. "Malla gets around the government rules that students must have a certain amount of exercise time every day. The way she does it is to wait until they have been out playing for a few minutes. Then she gives a tug on the chapel bell without letting the teachers even know she is going to do it. When the children get settled in chapel, she leads them in singing, reads a few verses from the Bible, and then gives a short devotional talk. Then it's over. It isn't long, but just long enough to interrupt the play time."

Another missionary added his explanation of Malla's determination to emphasize education. "She sees—as we all do—the many leaders of the church who were trained in mission schools. She knows that the future of the church depends on having trained members. In fact, some of the government leaders were educated in mission schools. That doesn't mean they are believers always, but many of them have heard the gospel. So, at her advanced age, Malla is still alert to visit the schools, pray with the teachers, and inspire the boys and girls to be saved and walk with the Lord. And she keeps writing to people at home to send money for more buildings. We need her."

Malla could never resist a chance to travel to other stations to see old friends and get aquainted with new missionaries. She no longer looked scornfully at cars, since they took her quickly to places that had once taken many days to reach by foot. Shortly before her eighty-ninth birthday, she heard that a woman witch doctor had accepted the Lord as Savior and was going to burn all her objects of witchcraft. The woman wanted the missionaries to be at the ceremony to share her gladness at being set free from years of demon worship.

"I must go," Malla exclaimed. "In all years I spend in Africa, I have not seen such a thing. I go, too, and tell her God set *me* free long years ago."

In spite of her frequent trips to mission stations and to kraals, Malla always wanted to be home at Bethel when new missionaries came through so she could cook them a welcome-to-Africa meal. She exclaimed, "I think God must love Africans. He sending so many new workers."

Malla often visited Emma Dawson, and she was always welcome. They had come to Africa together in the first tiny group of Scandinavian Alliance missionaries and had seen it become the great TEAM, The Evangelical Alliance Mission. They had been strangers together in a foreign land, sometimes sharing tears of homesickness. They had struggled to learn to eat unfamiliar food and to twist their tongues to make the difficult sounds of the Zulu language. They had shared in all that had gone into making missions work in South Africa. The frictions they had had in earlier years had been swallowed up in a deep friendship.

On one visit Malla came from her bedroom for morning tea, her face lighted by a smile. "Emma, listen. Sit down so I read to you, and you not do any work."

Malla sat down at the kitchen table, ignoring the steaming cup of tea Emma set before her. Her wrinkled fingers trembled as she tried to separate the thin pages of her Bible.

"Listen, Emma, to what God says. Here in Revelation 22, He says His servants will serve Him. Oh, Emma! How wonderful we not only serve here, but there too. You know, Emma, I have thought I wish I could live my life again. If I only young again, I think how much I could do yet. I think, when I die, I am through with work, and that make me sad. I never see this verse before that say I go on with work in heaven. That way we go on thanking for His so great love. Oh, that is wonderful!"

She looked across the room at Emma. "When we start out those long years ago, I tell God I serve Him to end of life. I not know then I live so long. I ask God maybe I go to heaven next month on ninetieth birthday."

Malla didn't make her trip into God's presence on her birthday. She had to wait a month longer before she went home to heaven. She finished her sixty-one-year tour of South Africa surrounded by her beloved black believers.